Legal Almanac Series No. 54

PRIVACY — ITS LEGAL PROTECTION

Based on Original Almanac
by

Hyman Gross

Revised Edition by
OCEANA EDITORIAL BOARD

1976
Oceana Publications, Inc.
Dobbs Ferry, New York

This is a revised edition of the fifty-fourth in a series of LEGAL ALMANACS which bring you the law on various subjects in nontechnical language. These books do not take the place of your attorney's advice, but they can introduce you to your legal rights and responsibilities.

Library of Congress Cataloging in Publication Data

Gross, Hyman.
    Privacy—its legal protection.

    (Legal almanac series; no. 54)
    Includes index.
    1. Privacy, Right of—United States—Popular works.
I. Title.
KF1262.Z9G7   1976   323.44   76-43110
ISBN 0-379-11099-7

Manufactured in the United States of America

TABLE OF CONTENTS

EDITOR'S NOTE TO THE SECOND EDITION vii

INTRODUCTION TO THE SECOND EDITION ... ix

INTRODUCTION TO THE FIRST EDITION xi

Chapter One — Privacy of Personality 1
  General Principles 1
    Invasion by Private Interests 1
    Use in the Public Interest 4
    Bounds of Public Interest 5
    Use Without Invasion 9
  Restricted Application 10
    What is a "Name" 10
    What is a "Picture" or "Portrait" 13
    What Are "Trade" or "Advertising" Purposes 14

Chapter Two — Facts of Life 18
  Biography 19
  Criminal Prosecutions 20
  Police Records 21
  Medical Data 21
  Debt Collection 22
  Shadowing and Surveillance 24
  Computers, Data Banks and Dossiers 25
  Credit Bureaus and Inspection Agencies 26
  Fair Credit Reporting Act of 1971 26
  Arrest Records 28
  The Direct Mail Industry 29
  Banks and Computerized Files 30

Chapter Three — Written Communication 32

  Mail 32

    Protection Against What Is Exposed 32

    Protection Against Prying 33

    Mail Watch 34

    Limits of Postal Protection 36

  Telegraph 37

    State Law 37

    Federal Law 38

  General Protective Provisions 39

Chapter Four — Spoken Communication 40

  Telephone Communication 41

    Nature of Federal Protection 41

    Protection Against What 44

    Who Is Protected 46

    State Protection 47

  Eavesdropping 48

    Constitutional Protection 48

    Statutory Protection 53

Chapter Five — Privilege to Withhold 54

  Privileged Subjects 55

  Privileged Communications 57

    General Principles 57

    Accountant and Client 57

    Journalist and Informant 58

    Clinical Psychologist and Client 59

    Attorney and Client 59

    Husband and Wife 60

    Doctor and Patient 62

    Religious Confessions and Communications 63

Chapter Six — Confidential Information 65

  Trade Secrets 65

    What Qualifies 65

    Role of Patent and Copyright 67

Protection Against What 68

Excluded Persons 69

Employees 70

Remedies 72

Confidential Business Facts 72

Entrusted Information 73

Confidential Disclosures to Government 74

Chapter Seven — Right to Be Secure 75

What Is Secured 77

   The Person 77

   The Place 78

   The Thing 79

Security for Whom 80

Violation of the Right 83

   What Is a Search 83

   Private Intrusions 84

   Arrest 85

   Inspections 85

   Orders to Produce for Examination 86

Protection of the Right 87

   Warrant 87

   Remedial Measures 88

**Chapter Eight — Privacy—From Property Right to
Personal Right** 90

Technology and Privacy 90

After Katz and Berger 95

National Security 96

Personal Privacy — Expanding the Concept 97

Privacy and Personal Choice — Roe v. Wade 99

Technology and Civil Liberty 100

The Privacy Act of 1974 106

Index 107

EDITOR'S NOTE TO THE SECOND EDITION

The original edition of this work, prepared in 1964 by Hyman Gross, dealt almost totally with the common law approach to privacy, as reinforced by statutory enactments in the states. Since that time, what was then the beginning suggestion that computer technology, data processing, and electronic surveillance would create significant legal issues, has evolved into a constitutional issue of major proportions, brought to a head in the Watergate crisis. The material that has been added to this volume deals largely with those issues in the context of cases determined by the U.S. Supreme Court and federal legislation such as the Fair Credit Reporting Act of 1971 and the Privacy Act. of 1974. Implicit in the development of this whole new body of law has been the recognition by the Supreme Court that the Fourth Amendment and its proscription against unwarranted search and seizure protects not only "property" rights, but "personal" rights, and that the physical intrusion on a man's premises is not the test of the Fourth Amendment, but rather any intrusion without proper authority, whether physical or otherwise.

In organizing this edition, the essential text of the original work, setting out the common law, has been preserved, and the examination of the newer issues and the newer law has been superimposed as additional material. While the new edition is the work of the editorial staff at Oceana Publications, the contribution of significant material by Ann Davies, Assistant Librarian at the Pappas Law Library, Boston University, is acknowledged with appreciation.

INTRODUCTION TO THE SECOND EDITION

One of the fundamental considerations in a free society must be the balancing of claims between the individual and the social order. This perpetual balancing expresses itself in a dynamic tension between individuals, constantly seeking to enlarge and expand the property-based notion of privacy and the state, which seeks the means to protect the society at large.

The earlier edition of this volume, published in 1964, dealt with those issues of privacy that had been subject to court hearings and decisions and have been recognized either in common law doctrines or in specific judicial decisions. These areas of privacy relate to such considerations as public interest, appropriation of names or pictures, search and seizure, privileged communications, trade secrets and other traditional issues.

In 1890, two young lawyers published an article in the *Harvard Law Review* called "The Right to Privacy". Warren and Brandeis argued that the common law had evolved slowly but steadily from physical protection of person and property to protection of personal rights and privacy, which they called "the right to be let alone." They concluded that the common law contained within it protection of the right to privacy, which could be extended to include not only the traditional definitions of personal privacy but the threat to that privacy caused by new mechanical devices such as cameras and recording machinery.

The right to be let alone has been further imperiled in the years since that classic article was written by the development of an immensely sophisticated technology, expressed by computers, elegant wiretap devices and electronic surveillance techniques. To those concerned with the preservation of civil liberties, technology poses an awesome threat to established constitutional guarantees. At the same time, the courts have recognized a constitutional right of privacy in the areas of purely personal choice such as contraception and abortion.

Privacy is virtually impossible to define in strictly legal terms. It varies with the times, the historical context, the state of the culture and the prevailing judicial philosophy. In our time the emphasis has shifted from a physical and property basis to a personal liberty basis. As a function of this conceptual shift has come vigorous legal action in the areas of electronic surveillance, data banks, credit reporting, bank secrecy, personal privacy and many other related concerns that will be touched on in this book.

The fundamental issues of personal freedom against state interest in regulating individual behavior form the consistent theme in privacy cases. Whether the specific question involves freedom of speech, the use of contraceptives, the right to have an abortion, or to wear one's hair at any desired length, there is usually a question of whether a compelling public interest should prevail over personal choice or whether personal liberties should control over an asserted state interest.

It will never again be possible to engage in any discussion of privacy without bringing in the Watergate affair. Watergate precipitated the first presidential resignation in American history and in doing so unveiled for endless public debate events in which the government itself violated the most basic prohibitions against invasion of privacy and later tried to justify them by citing "national security" as an overriding state interest. In that complex affair various intrusions were committed: bugging, taping of conversations, wiretapping, illegal entry. It is a veritable museum of constitutional violations. The operative Supreme Court decision in *Nixon v. Sirica* deals with the question of the constitutional powers of the president to invoke national security as a smokescreen for obvious intrusions upon, and invasions of, the privacy of both groups and individuals.

The earlier edition of this book discussed privacy and its legal protections as the record stood in 1964. The years since that time have seen more judicial activity in the area of the definition and enlargement of the concept of privacy than at any other time in our constitutional history. Older and more traditional applications will be discussed as a function of the general history of privacy. The larger part of this discussion will be devoted to the events of the last ten years and what the implications are for the daily cultural and political life of Americans.

INTRODUCTION TO THE FIRST EDITION

This book is about intrusions, usually uninvited and always unwelcome. It is concerned with the curiously civilized notion that getting to know things about people, and making them known to others, can be wrong. It examines how the law has received the idea that each person may reserve important areas of his life to himself.

The intrusions come in two forms: they may be the solemn acts of constituted authority professing the common welfare; or they may be the activities of other members of the community whose curiosity, though less authoritative, is no less insistent.

Inevitably, the social conditions of human life do impose limitations on the enjoyment of privacy. An important part of life in any human community is knowing what's going on, and the most important news is about people. Certain persons become the focus of the ambitions, appetites, and hopes that pervade the community, some for a day, some for a. lifetime or longer. Their names and images, and the details of their lives are eagerly responded to. The more private the facts of a public figure's life, the more interest they generate.

There is ample attention reserved for persons whose activities meet with disapproval in the community. Those disposed to violate rules which the community is disposed to enforce become objects of careful scrutiny. The police exist primarily for purposes of surveillance and detection, which are direct assaults on privacy.

Most people are not celebrities or criminals, but privacy is an issue in everyone's life. The avenues of social intercourse traveled in business and personal activities are places where interests compete. The interest in excluding others from knowledge of one's affairs comes into conflict with the interest others have in knowing what's going on, perhaps to satisfy curiosity, or for security or the enhancement of property or reputation.

It is obvious that legal protection of privacy is confronted at the outset with challenges presented by other interests entitled to legal recognition.

Further, a great many instances of privacy invasion lack sufficient objective importance to warrant legal intervention, and an awareness of this underlies judicial and legislative caution when acknowledgement and vindication of rights of privacy are sought. Depriving trivial and frivolous claims of the benefits of the legal process is necessary not only to promote expeditious administration of the law, but to keep our legal system in its proper place. The law does not aim at making rules for the minutiae of human affairs, but seeks to avoid such regulation in the interest of a free society. To enlarge, not diminish, the area of conflict of interests in which legal regulation is not necessary is the ideal of an open society. We seek to assert and balance our rights and to compose our differences outside the law. We guard against the growth of the law in a direction which, at an absurd extremity, would provide our neighbor with a legal cause against us for looking at him more intently than he would like, and recognize that each legal right asserted by one person is a limitation on the freedom of another.

It is important that invasions of privacy which constitute serious affronts to human dignity and threats to security receive legal attention. A man's life is a source of pride and dignity only when it is ultimately his own business. But there is reason in proceeding slowly with legal prohibition of petty harassments and humiliations. There are even more important things than privacy at stake—the ideals of a free society. Not the law, but the aroused conscience of the community should protect privacy in the first instance.

It is a commonplace observation that those communities which have the most extensive penal laws are not those which have the least crime. In most instances the opposite is the case. Prolix laws usually result from great needs, but pure volume of laws does not make for enforcement. The existence of laws and the degree to which they are respected are two different matters, and there is little reason to hope that more elaborate legal regulation in the interest of privacy will promote greater respect for rights of privacy, anymore than a mass of penal laws will reduce crime.

Legal terms maintain roots in the fertile soil of ordinary speech, but have their own principles of development. Difficulties arise when the erratic range of common usages of a term such as "privacy" is imported into the legal process. For one thing, it appears that established legal concepts such as trespass, nuisance, defamation, and others, developed with precision in a body of rules, are to be replaced by some ill-defined embryonic notion. For another, there appears to be no bounds to the areas in which privacy may be found, and for which legal protection is sought. It is necessary, therefore, to distinguish the concept of privacy in the law from other concepts which lie behind various common uses of the term and which, on appropriate occasions, are recognized by the law in other forms.

A public address system in a railroad station broadcasts advertising (or perhaps just music). We say our privacy is invaded. A loudspeaker in the street broadcasts a political speech and we have the same complaint, but are less sure if we can restore silence by closing the window (provided closed windows are in season). Innumerable instances are at hand. In these cases privacy is conceived as *mental solitude*.

The government condemns ten acres of a fifteen-acre estate and appropriates the land for public housing. Privacy has been lost. But the loss is something quite different than in the previous case. In this instance it is *physical seclusion*.

Suppose the landlord demands a pass key for the lock installed by his tenant; or the chambermaid insists on coming in to clean the hotel room while the guest is performing his morning ablutions; or the fellow sharing a seat on the train reads along with his neighbor from the other's newspaper. Clearly privacy is at stake. Here, however, privacy is *power of exclusion*.

We speak of planning a family, choosing a school, or

attending church as being private matters. Anyone who would venture to decide or act for us in these things would be encroaching upon our privacy. Privacy in this case means *autonomy*.

In many situations more than one interest which we call privacy is challenged. When the telephone rings at home and the uninvited caller solicits business most people would agree that privacy is being interfered with. In this case there seem to be two interests affected: an interest in remaining undisturbed (mental solitude); and in not having untoward intrusions into the enjoyment of life at home (exclusion). A letter under the door at home for the same purpose would touch on privacy as exclusion, but not as solitude; while the same phone call to reach a prospect at his club would affect solitude but not any exclusionary interest (unless, of course, the club was also home).

The interest in privacy which receives recognition *as such* in the law is the subject of this book. It is expressed in the reply "I'm sorry, but that's my business." The remark might naturally come to the lips of anyone expressing his claim to privacy in connection with a matter covered in any chapter of this book.

In the chapters to follow we look at areas of life in which a right to privacy has received acknowledgement. The considerations to be borne in mind throughout are the same. What is the interest recognized by the law? What principles limit the existence and enjoyment of the right?

One reason for refusing to protect privacy is its abandonment by the one claiming protection. A course of conduct or a way of life which makes a person a public figure puts an end to his privacy, at least for what is put in the public domain. Disclosures, whether explicitly made or resulting from some course of conduct, are a surrender of privacy. But a disclosure in confidence or under special conditions to one person or a restricted group does place limitations on the loss of privacy.

Another way to lose rights of privacy is by the abuse of

privacy. Criminal acts require secrecy in their planning and execution, and to avoid detection afterward. Protection of persons and property in the community requires interference with the privacy of criminals. But what about the privacy of one merely suspected of criminal activity, or one suspected only of planning a crime? At what point shall suspicions alone, without evidence of criminal acts, be sufficient justification for denying rights of privacy? And are there activities other than criminal which are an abuse of privacy justifying intrusion by the community?

There are many valuable interests which conflict with privacy. Free speech to one man is unwanted disclosure to another. Telling the news may involve unwanted publicity. Business ventures may involve ascertaining facts which others prefer to remain unknown. Ways must be found to weigh competing interests to determine which are entitled to protection. It is only for very good cause that the exercise of freedom to see, to learn, to speak, should entail legal peril. We do not aim for a mute and ignorant condition, but rather an informed and articulate community.

When weighing privacy in balance with other interests, certain sorts of considerations are given attention to determine how weighty is in fact the interest in privacy in a particular case.

The *consequences* of an invasion of privacy are looked to. Is there injury to something which we would be inclined to treat as a kind of property, such as the commercial value of a name or picture or business information? The acquaintance of the law with these kinds of injuries is a certain one, and protection is therefore more readily available. Is the injury to dignity, a cheapening of image, a loss of stature by the very fact of publicity? These are the most difficult cases, the law hesitating most when the harm claimed is publication itself. In between are cases where the injury is apparent mental suffering, such as humiliation resulting from observation or disclosure of intimacies.

Motives are important. Courts will regard very differently the same acts of invasion when in one instance they are maliciously conceived to embarrass the victim, and in another pursued altruistically for general social benefit. These are the extremes of motivation. In between lie situations where some selfish interest is the motive, such as a desire for profit from an otherwise lawful enterprise; or the limited altruism which is present when benefit is conferred on a limited segment of the community with whom the actor has some connection, such as a protective association and the members it serves.

The *methods* employed are very persuasive. The law protects against deceptions, violence, betrayals, sneakiness, and illegality. Violations of privacy are often accomplished by fraud (such as misrepresenting the true purpose for which information is sought); or by physical or mental abuse (an issue most frequently, though by no means exclusively, raised in connection with police methods); or by exploiting positions of confidence which one has accepted or insinuated oneself into; or by stealth (such as stealing papers, but including any violation which would be difficult or impossible to accomplish if the victim knew what was going on); or by acts which constitute other crimes, such as extortion. Such means weigh heavily against the interests in which they are employed, and enhance the standing of the victim.

Preliminary mapping is completed, and detailed examination in order. Throughout the chapters which follow, emphasis is placed on issues, not rules. This seemed especially appropriate in areas where the law is largely emergent at the present time. The customary trappings of legal presentation have been omitted to conform with the non-technical format of the Legal Almanac Series.

Chapter 1

PRIVACY OF PERSONALITY

GENERAL PRINCIPLES

Names and likenesses of persons are latecomers to the field of legal protection. Except when a person's reputation or economic interests were threatened, the use of his name or image imposed no legal liability. Personality, which is trespassed upon by the very *use* of these extensions of personality, was not recognized as a proper subject for legal concern. Such recognition began in this country at the turn of the century, and its status is still more or less in doubt in more than half the states. Twenty have given clear recognition, while four have explicitly denied it.

Invasion by Private Interests

In Alabama a person well known in the sports world was successful in claiming that his privacy was invaded when a broadcasting company advertised that he would be announcing its football programs. In fact, he had made no firm arrangements with the broadcaster. Quite apart from the truth of falsity of the advertised statement, the court said that being a person well known to the public did not entail abandonment of a right to restrict public use of one's name, at least where the matters in connection with which it is used are not happenings which invite publicity.

A California attorney was sustained in his contention that the use of his name in a copying machine advertisement, though only one among hundreds of names of supposedly satisfied customers, was a violation of a right of privacy. The fact that he was distinctly dissatisfied with the machine and the advertiser knew it, was irrelevant. The unauthorized use of his name was enough.

In Louisiana, an accident victim successfully objected that his privacy was invaded by an advertisement prepared and inserted by his insurance company. The advertisement was in the form of a plea to anyone who witnessed the accident to come forward as a witness, and bore the signature of the insured victim. All of this was done without the knowledge of the victim.

California, whose courts are often presented with exceptional specimens of entrepreneurial invention, produced the case of a woman who claimed that her privacy was invaded by a mailing consisting of a thousand letters, designed to promote a new motion picture. The letters were written in a feminine hand on feminine stationery and were signed with the plaintiff's name. It was also the name of the picture's female lead character. The letter proposed a rendezvous at the theater in a way leaving no doubt as to its intended object. The letters were mailed to a select list of males in the community. As it happened, the plaintiff was the only woman in the local phone book with this name, and the response she received indicated a highly successful mailing. The court found that this mailing constituted an invasion of privacy even though only the names, and not the persons named, were identical, and though there was no intention by the architects of the promotional scheme that the plaintiff be thought to be the author of the letter.

The use of a man's name in a product name or endorsement was restrained in New Jersey as violative of rights of privacy, and the restriction extended to use of his name in the manufacturing corporation's name. In this case, the person protected was world famous (Thomas Edison); protection of privacy here was protection against illicit use, not publicity.

A court in Oklahoma denied relief to a motion picture producer whose curious contention was that a right of privacy was violated by the denial of publicity. Among his other grievances, he claimed that advertising displays by local theaters failed to mention certain names, and displayed others without due prominence, thereby invading the private realm of those whose names were neglected. The court did not agree that lack of publicity or badly executed publicity is an invasion of privacy, and held, furthermore, that the free use made of names and pictures was proper since names and faces of stars (and their producers) are sold to the public along with the motion picture.

In Ohio, a nominating petition for public office was published in a newspaper. A signer brought suit, claiming invasion of privacy. The court denied the claim on the ground that the petition was a public document open to public inspection, and newspaper publication merely facilitated this.

In Texas, it was held that a football star could not object that a violation of his privacy was constituted by the use of his picture on a calendar advertising beer because his picture was already well known to the public, and the use of the picture was not as an endorsement by him of the product.

This case does not accord recognition to rights which are generally recognized by other courts. When a person becomes a public personality he is that for public purposes, but not for the private purpose of selling beer. And when his picture is placed on an advertising piece its purpose is to help sell the product, whether or not he is depicted endorsing the product. It is not a right to compensation for the use which is being asserted in the legal action, but a right to compensation for loss of privacy resulting from commercial usage.

The cases so far have all involved publication to the general public or some part of it. This is not necessary, however.

A false impersonation of a businessman in a telephone call to the businessman's regular supplier by others anxious to get his business was held, in Georgia, to be a use of the businessman's name which violated his right of privacy.

Signing a man's name to a telegram (opposing pending legislation) which was prepared and sent to the Governor without the man's consent was held a violation of his privacy in Oregon.

Consent to the use of one's picture by another normally limits the use to the person to whom consent is granted. Thus in a Michigan case a model who posed for her employer was successful in a suit against a department store that bought the picture from the photographer and used it to advertise the store's merchandise. In Indiana, a lens grinder, whose picture had been used for morale publicity by the Army during his service career, succeeded in an action brought against an optical company who copied the picture and used it in its advertising.

Consent to a use is effective for a reasonable time, after which rights of privacy are restored. So in Louisiana the court decided that republication ten years later of "before-and-after" pictures for a body-building course was a violation of privacy. The model was presumably a considerably changed person, both in body and sensibilities, and suffered embarrassment from remarks of acquaintances who saw the ad.

Use in the Public Interest

One who is involved in a happening of public interest, even if accidentally, loses his rights of privacy in that connection. A man who happened to be standing at the counter of a store when it was raided by police in Florida and was shown prominently on a televised clip of the incident shortly after, was denied damages when he sued the broadcaster for invasion of privacy.

Occurrences of a quasi-private sort have been recognized as privileged. In Minnesota, courtroom photographs of a domestic relations proceeding were published in the paper. It was held that although the proceeding was civil, not criminal, it could still be a proper subject of public interest and since no unusual use was made of the picture by the accompanying story no right of privacy was violated.

Subsequent events often recall earlier ones, and a present triviality can be sufficient as a pretext to recall something of public interest. A radio "life-sketch" of a man who disappeared and was mistakenly thought murdered, was broadcast twenty-five years later when he died. An Alabama court found the whole story newsworthy, and not a violation of privacy rights.

Present obscurity, even with the absence of any present event as a pretext to penetrate it, is no shield against publicity.

A former child prodigy, once in the public eye but living for over twenty years in obscurity, was held to be an unprotected subject for a magazine piece about his subsequent eccentric life. A privilege is enjoyed for news or matters of general interest, which the court found to be present here, and obscure doings may be as interesting as prominent ones.

Public officials have no right of privacy with regard to their conduct in public office. In a case under Indiana law, this was held to continue beyond the time of office-holding, so that a highly embarrassing picture of a prosecutor taken with the famous criminal John Dillinger fifteen years before could be republished as a matter still within the public interest. Here the occasion was a feature article of the "what's become of them" variety. The article's current pretext had nothing to do with the unfortunate ex-prosecutor.

Bounds of Public Interest

Use in the public interest must be just that to justify the sacrifice of privacy. Where the purposes are primarily selfish ones, or other considerations determine the use to be not in the public interest, the rights of privacy prevail.

California had a pair of cases based on the same photograph published in two different magazines, *The Ladies Home Journal* and *Harper's Bazaar*. The photographer, the world famous Cartier-Bresson, took a picture of a married couple who owned and managed an ice cream concession in a leading shopping complex. The husband had his arm around his wife's waist in a romantic pose. The picture appeared without consent in the *Journal* as part of an article on love, and was used to illustrate what the article said was the most dangerous kind—love based on sexual attraction alone. The court found that the fact that this scene was enacted in a public place did not deprive it of its limited privacy, which was destroyed by world-wide magazine publication; and the fact that the subject of the article—love— was of general interest did not afford license for this sort of publication, since the privilege of public interest extends only to what the public is interested in—in this case love, not the romantic couple. The second case involved an inoffensive use of the picture as an illustration for a "love makes the world go round" article. The court, though not without sharp dissent, backed up and found that the publication did not violate rights of privacy because whatever offense to the sensibilities of the couple there was resulted from their voluntary act of affection in a public place, and was not enlarged by the publication as in the first case. The court expressed concern that any persons appearing anywhere in any published picture would have a claim if the plantiff's in this instance was upheld. The core of the distinction appears to be the distortion which the *Journal* article perpetrates, thereby depriving that use of the privilege available to a medium of communication and information.

A reformed prostitute, accused and acquitted in a sensational and widely publicized murder trial seven years before, had since married and lived a life of respectable obscurity. A motion picture account of the crime used her real unmarried name in portraying her earlier life. Violation of privacy was found by a California court, indicating that lost privacy, like lost virtue, can be recovered and can again become the subject of protection. The film was nothing more than a commercial venture, and so without privilege for the harm it caused.

A radio crime serial which depicted an actual robbery, using the victim's real name, was held in California to violate the victim's right of privacy. Again, only a commercial purpose was found to exist.

The *Saturday Evening Post* published an article critical of taxi drivers in the nation's capital. One illustration was a picture of a woman hackie. The court, in finding an invasion

6

of her privacy, thought that the article went beyond the sort whose primary purpose is information, since the presentation was very flamboyant and the primary object obviously satire. Though the author's criticism may have been just, most people would not be likely to describe the piece as simply a presentation of facts with critical comment. It was, therefore, not within the privilege.

An important issue was presented in a Florida case in which a Pulitzer Prize author was sued by an acquaintance portrayed in a book about life in a backwoods area of the state, previously quite unknown. The defense spared no effort or expense to show how meritorious the literary achievements of the defendant were, and how as a result of her writings the region had acquired a measure of fame in which its inhabitants shared as subjects of nationwide and worldwide interest. The court accepted these facts, and then concluded that rights of privacy had indeed been violated. It was the defendant, by her writings, not the events of the world or the doings of the plaintiff by herself that made the plaintiff an object of public curiosity. The rationale of this decision is of great importance in affording for privacy protection against publicity ventures which seek first to create a public interest, and then to exploit it.

The circumstances under which a thing is acquired, particularly with reference to pictures, may affect its privilege.

Time ran an article captioned "Starving Glutton." A woman had entered a hospital in Missouri complaining that she couldn't stop eating. Reporters talked to her, and while she protested that she wanted no publicity her photograph was surreptitiously snapped and later printed with a story about how she ate enough for ten people but kept losing weight. The court said the fact that people would be interested to know about a person in these strange circumstances did not confer privilege on the magazine. Public curiosity was not enough. If what people were interested in were the test, as *Time* contended it should be, the intimate details of all our lives would have no legal protection provided only that they were intimate enough to insure public interest. The crucial fact for this decision was the unconsented to, **and** indeed resisted, violation of a hospital patient's seclusion **by** the press trying to get a story.

A Pennsylvania decision concerns photographs taken **of** an unconscious hospital patient by a doctor. The pictures were taken for legitimate medical purposes, though not necessary to the patient's treatment. No consent from the patient or her husband was obtained. The court decided that the sacrifice of privacy in the interest of medical science is a matter within the patient's, not the doctor's discretion, and ordered the negatives and all prints to be surrendered.

A photograph of a woman suicide was stolen from **her** home and reproduced in a local paper reporting the story in California. Whatever else this may have constituted, the court held the publication was not an invasion of privacy, because the event was intrinsically newsworthy.

A number of cases have held, however, that reprehensible means employed to obtain a photograph destroy the privilege which would otherwise exist for its publication. In all such cases, the picture was not used as part of live news coverage (as in the previous case), but for feature article purposes.

Questions of decency or propriety are sometimes raised, and it is contended that no public interest is served when there is publication of a scene which falls below minimum standards.

A shocking picture of a girl of eleven lying in a public street, mutilated, and with limbs indecently exposed, accompanied a newspaper account of an accident. A Pennsylvania court refused to recognize this as an invasion of privacy, saying that the court will not concern itself with canons of taste and that as long as the bounds of obscenity are not crossed, the picture is privileged as news.

Another case decided under Pennsylvania law involved publication in a detective story magazine of a picture of a man who had been kicked to death by a gang two months previous to the publication. The court found there was **no** right of privacy, even for the members of the victim's family whose pictures also appeared, since the incident was still a matter of public interest. The court made the points that public interest may be in information or entertainment; and that the court will not withhold privilege from material within the range of public interest because of considerations of taste, or worth of the material, or the sort of gratification intended, unless it is obscene or otherwise legally infamous.

An elaborate national network of police records is maintained and continually enlarged in the interest of law enforcement. The question of police photographs of a person arrested and what may be done about them if there is a subsequent acquittal, has been raised in cases in a number of states. The prevailing authority is that the police are free to exercise their discretion in deciding whose picture and fingerprints shall be destroyed and whose retained in identification files, regardless of the outcome of proceedings after arrest, and regardless of the person's reputation and position in the community. However, any improper use of such material retained in the file of a person who is released, such as exhibition in a "rogue's gallery" to identify suspects, will be prohibited as an invasion of privacy. There is some authority that photographing and fingerprinting upon arrest may be prevented if the nature of the charge and the circumstances of the accused indicate clearly that there is no public necessity for this humiliating procedure.

Use Without Invasion

There are limits to the kind of use which is an invasion of privacy. Names and pictures may be used for a great variety of purposes which do not affect privacy, or looking at it from another angle, do not involve the use of a personality.

A father sued an insurance company in South Carolina, claiming that his right of privacy was violated when the company issued a policy on his life to his son as beneficiary, but without his consent. He said that his name had been used for commercial purposes, and that this was violative of his rights. The court decided that privacy could not be invaded by mere use, without communication to others, which was the situation here.

A news photograph of a racing accident was reprinted in a fiction magazine. An Illinois court found that no identification of the driver, either directly or through identification of the car, could be made from the picture, and only independent knowledge of the event could be a basis of identification. In this instance there was no violation of rights of privacy since the picture did not make use of a personality.

RESTRICTED APPLICATION

New York recognizes no common-law right of privacy, but has a statute which is designed to protect against invasions in this area. Three other states—Virginia, Oklahoma, and Utah—have enacted similar legislation, with coverage extended to names and pictures of dead persons as well as living.

A large volume of cases has been brought under the New York statute, testing and sharpening the general principles previously outlined in this chapter. The terms of the statute restrict the latitude of protection, but as we shall see, the same underlying principles are regarded by New York courts. This has necessitated nimble circumlocution in the face of the express terms of the statute. These terms have been stretched, as a result, to a point where their meanings can be determined only by a reading of the cases in which the terms are applied, with careful attention to the peculiar facts of each.

The statute prohibits the use of the name, picture, or portrait of a living person for purposes of trade or advertising without his written consent. Violation is a misdemeanor, and civil remedies are available in the form of restraining injunction for threatened use, or damages for uses already made.

What is a "Name"

Names can be made up or abandoned. Part of a name may do the job of naming; and one name may be included in another. Most important, the use of a name might be mention of a particular person who bears that name, but then again it might not be. If not, there is not a use of the name of *that* particular person.

These facts about names present problems for the application of the statute.

The scion of a famous Italian noble family sued a wine company for using the family name and coat of arms as a decoration on its labels, claiming that it was the equivalent of using his name since he was the oldest living member of the family. The court held that this action was a proper one under the statute, although the plaintiff would have to prove that in fact the designation on the label identified *him* in the mind of the public viewing it.

An obscure attorney was denied relief on his claim that his name had been used for trade purposes in a novel. His last name, somewhat uncommon, had been used throughout as the name of a minor character who was a lawyer; and his first name was also the same as the fictional character's, but appeared only once in the book. The court found there were no other similarities, no extrinsic evidence of an intention to use the real person, and so no commercial purpose indicated by the facts. This does not mean, however, that "purposes of trade" includes only those uses which are profitable to the user. The fact that any other name used would serve the purposes at hand equally well is not a defense. The purpose of the use, not its value, is what entitles the name to protection under the statute.

The novel and film *From Here to Eternity* raised a similar question. A person with the same last name as one of the characters, who had served in the Army with the author, claimed the benefit of the statute. The name was not uncommon, and the details of the plaintiff's army service bore no significant resemblance to those of the character. The court did not agree that there was sufficient identification, and saw no evidence of a trade purpose which might have been pursued in using this particular person as the prototype.

When a cartoonist living in Chicago was sued by a Georgia couple of whose existence he was unaware, but who had

11

the same name as his comic-strip characters, the court dismissed the action. It said that the name used must be intended to be a particular person's in order for such person to invoke the statute. Absent any knowledge of the existence of the particular people such intention is impossible.

In one case, the court decided that use of a family name in a corporation's name could not be restrained, since it was unlikely that the person complaining would be thought of when the corporate name was mentioned, and since there was no showing that anything unfair or harmful to the person would result from such use.

The use of a name may be merged in the use of a thing which it accompanies so that the name no longer is a distinct element in the use. The name, in such a case, is not a token of personality and not an intended object of the statute's protection.

Where there was no protection of a dress design, the dress could be copied and sold with the name of the original designer indicated. The same approach was taken in the case of a signed architect's rendering in which the client had rights of reproduction, and which was incorporated in an advertisement by the client with the architect's signature clearly appearing.

Where a news clipping with a tennis star's name was reproduced on a fabric, the court held that this was an innocent occurrence of the name. A dissenting opinion said that if the name was found to have any significance in enhancing the commercial value of the fabric, protection should be available.

A fictitious or stage name, in this case "Aunt Jemima," was held to come within the bounds of the statute, since there was widespread identification of a particular performer by that name. The court did recognize limitations on when use of such a name might be restricted since it is in the public domain. And the right cannot be asserted against someone who has prior rights in the name as, for example, by trademark registration.

Yankee Doodle Dandy presented a case where considerable liberties were taken in a film account of the life of a famous songwriter. His former wife came out of European seclusion to claim that her privacy had been violated under the statute, although the film includes no mention of her name or anything approximating an accurate portrayal of her. Instead the picture substituted an almost completely fictional wife. The court found no violation of privacy, since there was insufficient grounds for establishing identity between the real person and the film character. The only thing of importance which the two shared was the marital title, "Mrs. George M. Cohan."

Another sort of "artificial" name is a trade-name, usually applied to a product or business enterprise. Where a person's name was used as part of a trade-name, was well-known and of obvious commercial value, the court found an intention to exploit the person's identity commercially, and granted relief.

The right conferred by the statute has been held not to protect the names of corporations and partnerships, and trade-names. Privacy of personality is a matter of concern to natural persons only, and the statute's coverage is limited accordingly.

What is a "Picture" or "Portrait"

It is apparent that the purposes of this law would not be served by restricting its application to the products of photographers and painters, or, indeed, to visual representations generally. Equally undesirable would be inclusion in its coverage of instances where a personality does not survive in the finished product, although an ingredient in the process of its creation.

A model employed by a department store posed for a "sculpture" reproduction of her face and body to be immortalized as a mannikin. Without her consent the mannikin was put into mass production and sold. The court found that the three-dimensional likeness was embraced by the statute as fully as any two-dimensional verisimilitude would be.

However, a sailor who posed for a Navy poster was held

to have been only raw material which the artist used in creating an original idealized figure, therefore not entitled to the protection of the statute. In deciding this the court acknowledged that the poster image was recognizable as the sailor. This decision is made to turn on the question of whether the poster is a picture of the plaintiff, or whether the plaintiff was simply used to create an original picture in which he, as an ingredient, is still recognizable. In the latter case there is not a use of personality, but only use of the services of a person. Privacy is not at issue.

A portrayal need not be such that visual recognition of the person portrayed is possible. A film, made almost entirely in a studio by actors depicting the actual heroic deeds of a ship's telegrapher during a shipwreck, was held to be using a "portrait" of the hero, despite the fact that the appearance of the film character was different from that of the person portrayed.

The novel and play *A Bell for Adano* precipitated a claim by a former military government officer that a leading character was modeled after him. The court said that there was no intention that the statute cover situations where acts and events portrayed in fiction corresponded to those in the lives of real persons. A dissenting opinion argued that if indeed a real person is portrayed in fiction this constitutes a use for purposes of trade, and the fact that a made-up name is given the character does not significantly affect the portrayal. The issue which divided the court was really one of determining when a personality is being used: is a portrayal of certain acts of a person, and of certain occurrences in his life, enough to constitute a portrait of that person; or must there be mention of things which uniquely identify him.

What Are "Trade" or "Advertising" Purposes

The public interest in information and free communication, which is held to be paramount to individual interests in privacy, is what really determines which uses are not "for purposes of trade or advertising" under the statute. It is not contribution to profits resulting from a use about which the courts inquire. Rather they are concerned with exploitation of a name or likeness, because this is a sacrifice of privacy for some selfish end rather than for a public necessity. Whether such exploitation is found to exist depends upon subject matter and manner of presentation.

A book about professional strikebreakers, replete with pictures and extensive biographical material, was determined to be published for purposes of edification rather than trade.

When *Confidential Magazine* published a story accompanied by pictures concerning intimate details in the life of a socially prominent man and his wife, the court decided that his prominence had already destroyed his privacy, and that even highly sensational treatment of the subject will not imperil the immunity of a publication giving the public what it is interested in getting. The court will not evaluate the interest of the public, but simply respect the fact of it.

It might be well to recall at this point that privacy, not reputation, is the thing claimed to be harmed in all these cases. If the articles in question can be shown to be defamatory in an action for libel, that is quite another matter.

A case which involved a picture was the occasion of a further refinement of the public interest privilege. A newspaper ran a feature article on the Indian rope trick to accompany a news story on a prize offered by a British society interested in occult matters. The plaintiff was depicted as a Hindu musician in an illustration which was part of the article. The court's holding was that such articles were like those about travel, or the lives of interesting people, or interesting historical events. They are essentially educational and so privileged, and to be distinguished from fabrications whose value lie in invention, not communication.

Use of name and picture in an "inquiring photographer" column in a newspaper has been held not a use for "trade" purposes.

In a case which sharply divided the court, the majority held that a comic-strip version of a real person who had been the hero of the Empire State Building airplane disaster

15

six months before was not violative of rights under the statute. This was on the theory that there was a continuing public interested in the event which was recounted in comic-strip form. The dissenting opinion took the position that such treatment went beyond the bounds of public interest and clearly was use of the name and image of the plaintiff for trade purposes.

A biography of a famous conductor was written and published without his authorization. The court held that he had no grounds for claiming the protection of the statute since the book was not a fictionalized treatment of his life and did not distort or misrepresent. The biography was an instance of dissemination of information and comment.

The name and picture of an amateur lady sleuth could be used with impunity in a feature film made from newsreels shortly after the newsworthy events in which she was involved. But a courtroom news photograph could not be republished some years later in a magazine feature article under a lurid caption.

Mere incidental use of a name in fiction or moving pictures is held not to be violative, since there is not the exploitation for trade which the statute envisages. Thus the single mention of a name in the course of the dialogue of a film, or in a press release attending it, or in a novel, or magazine article, have all been held to be innocent under the statute. In other words the statute has been construed so as not to choke communication, but simply to prevent unwanted exploitation.

The widow and daughter of a songwriter about whose career a film had been made sued under the corresponding statute of Utah. Their claim was that the picture was a portrayal for trade purposes, and not, as the producer contended, a depiction of something of public interest entitled to the privilege accorded news and, possibly, educational films. They were successful, the court finding that the man's personality was appropriated by the film makers for an entertainment, and not purveyed to the public to satisfy curiosity or gratify some general interest.

Advertising uses of pictures present much clearer cases of

infringements upon rights of privacy because the profit motive of the user is pure and unalloyed. But news contained in an advertisement, when the "news" is of news interest, has been held to confer the same immunity for the use of names as on other occasions of news publication. When, however, the news item is stale and reproduced not to excite interest in the occurrence but in a product which is mentioned, the appearance of a person's name in the copy is an illicit use of the name.

When between-the-halves entertainment was televised as part of a football broadcast, the public event character of the game was held to free the broadcaster from liability to the half-time entertainer for uses interdicted by the statute. The crucial fact to be found was that the entertainment was given with knowledge that it was part of a public event. Privacy protected by the statute was surrendered when the entertainer voluntarily became part of the public event, and since the broadcast was coverage of a public event it was not exploitation for trade purposes.

Chapter 2

FACTS OF LIFE

In the last chapter we looked into the matter of protecting a person's identity. In this one we take up the matter of protection for things about a person. Here we are not concerned with use of a personality but with revelations about the person. The gist of compromising privacy through naming and depiction is exposure of personality. The facts of a person's life may be of interest because of who the person is. Sometimes, however, the nature of the facts make them matters of interest. Where such facts are important because of who the person is, it is again exploitation of a personality which is the issue. When the facts are interesting in themselves, it is the fact that they are part of someone's life which raises the issue of privacy.

When of the first sort the facts would be of no interest without an identification of the person. And even when the facts are interesting in themselves, they assume added realism when the identity of the person is supplied. Quite natturally, therefore, legal actions for violation of privacy by publication of facts about someone frequently do include claims based on the use of the person's name or picture. The interest at stake is, however, somewhat different. It is like the difference between knowing a person and knowing about him. The judicial emphasis is less upon preventing exploitation and more upon protecting sensibilities.

Some of the cases discussed in Chapter I have facts about people as the subject of the offending publicity. The same legal principles which are brought to bear when names and pictures are used are appropriate in these instances.

Biography

A biography is the specific vehicle for telling the story of a person's life. To what extent does the subject have rights which limit the biographer's freedom?

The famous conductor, Serge Koussevitzsky, was the subject of a biography which he refused to authorize. In holding that this work did not constitute a violation of a right of privacy, the New York court emphasized that the biography was not a fictionalized account. It dealt with matters in which he, as a person who had become a certain sort of public figure, might expect the public to be interested, and did not deal with intimate details of his personal life. Hence it did not fall within the bounds of the New York statute. In this case, of course, it was the use of the subject's name and picture which provided the technical basis of the claim under the statute (see *supra*, p. 10), but the real issue concerned the narration of the man's life and professional career. The book contained a considerable amount of unfavorable comment, as well as praise, and was by no means an uncritical factual account. It also contained a considerable number of doubtful anecdotes. Nevertheless the court maintained that the book was a legitimate dissemination of information in the public interest.

A biographical piece which takes much greater liberties in the treatment of its subject was a profile published in *The New Yorker* magazine. Its obvious purpose was entertainment, not information. The subject was a child prodigy who had lived his adult life somewhat eccentrically and in complete obscurity. The article was concerned principally with what had happened to him, dwelling on the strange failure of earlier promise. He had been born on April 1st, and the article's subtitle was "April Fool." The Federal Court of Appeals considered the matter under the New York statute and the laws of fourteen other states. The court extended the privilege of public interest to this article, maintaining that what had happened to a former subject of public interest was a matter of continuing public interest. Recognition was given to the possibility of revelations so intimate and unwarranted as to outrage the community's sense of decency. But this was not the case here, and the mores of the community was the standard by which the court thought it proper to abide.

Criminal Prosecutions

In a case brought in Federal District Court, in which the law in all the states was considered (since publication had been nationwide), the plaintiffs had been convicted of murder and the defendant magazine publisher had run a contemporaneous story on the case in a crime magazine. Included was mention of sexual relations which the plaintiffs were said to have had with each other. The conviction was subsequently reversed on appeal, and the accused were freed. They sued the magazine, claiming the story was an indecent, lurid presentation designed to serve the purposes of fiction, not of news or information. The court said that while unquestionably the accused had no right of privacy with regard to reports of the criminal charges, they did not surrender their rights of privacy in toto, and that if a jury found that the magazine treatment exceeded the bounds of decency in light of their subsequent discharge by the appellate court, then they could recover for invasion of privacy. The publishers were thus made to assume the risk in the changed circumstances resulting from the appeal. Just as privacy may, in some instances, be subsequently recovered, so the privilege to invade it with impunity may be extinguished by subsequent events. The unarticulated premise on which this decision is based is the notion that a lurid account of a crime exceeds the bounds of decency when the accused is acquitted, but not when convicted. It follows that if there is a conviction, such account of the crime will be privileged as a matter of public interest. If the accused are acquitted, such an account is found to offend canons of propriety prevailing in the community, and privilege is withheld.

A case brought in the District of Columbia made it clear

that a defendant in a criminal case becomes fair game, without recourse, for any newsworthy report or speculation about him. In this case a radio commentator reported that the defendant, charged with seditious conduct, might still overhear conversations of high government figures in the job he retained as a Washington bartender.

A California court considered the case of parents who had been subjected to publicity attendant upon the arrest and trial of their son who stood charged with unlawful assembly to watch a hot-rod race. He was acquitted. The defendants in this case were those officials responsible for the arrest and prosecution, and the court held that they could no more be held liable for publicity attending official acts of public interest than could those who report the events.

Police Records

Improper use of data in police files will be restrained by courts. Dissemination of information prior to conviction will normally be enjoined unless a person is a fugitive from justice. Once a person has been convicted, however, the range of proper uses for police information about him is greatly extended, or, perhaps more to the point, his rights of privacy are greatly diminished.

Medical Data

The privacy of medical data has been passed on in several cases concerned with photographs. A woman's pelvic region was shown in an illustration accompanying a newspaper article on the hazard of surgical hardware remaining inside after an operation. Under Oklahoma law it was held that the publisher was liable for invasion of privacy. In Pennsylvania, a doctor was restrained from using the photograph of a patient taken without her knowledge (see p. 8 *supra*). In New York, the patients' rights were recognized in two cases. The first was concerned with a deformed nose portrayed in a medical journal which, the court said, would violate the New York statute as a use for advertising if its purpose was publicity (for the doctor) rather than scientific information, which would be privileged. The

21

second case concerned the filming of a Caesarian delivery, consented to for medical purposes. The sequence was subsequently included in a film about birth which was made for commercial, not scientific, purposes. The trade purpose was apparent, and so a violation of privacy was found to exist even though the film was informational.

Debt Collection

There is one class of facts which never lacks attention. What a person owes is always the concern of the person to whom it is owed, and it is sometimes brought to the attention of others. Who these others are and what the circumstances of the disclosure are, determine the question of whether such communications are violations of privacy entitled to legal redress.

In Georgia a telegram was sent to the debtor demanding payment and threatening legal action. It was claimed that disclosure to Western Union by the creditor was a wrongful invasion of privacy. The court disagreed, saying it was a perfectly proper means of pursuing his interest in collection by the creditor.

Two Kentucky cases show what is beyond the allowed limits. In one, a newspaper published a notice in the form of a communication from grocer to customer stating how much was owed and for how long. Since such a method is designed to hold up the debtor to contempt, ridicule, and disgrace, and thereby coerce payment, no privilege was allowed to the publisher for this invasion. In another case, a large sign was posted in a prominent window of a garage. The same reasoning was followed by the court in finding for the complaining debtor and against his creditor.

A woman in Louisiana was recovering from a heart attack. An automobile dealer to whom she owed money called her doctor and asked if he thought it would be all right to go ahead with collection. This was answered in the negative. The woman sued the dealer, claiming her privacy had been violated by a disclosure of the debt to her doctor. The court found this a perfectly proper course of conduct under the circumstances, and denied recovery.

22

The largest cluster of cases in this area concern disclosures to employers of an employee's debt. Cases in Michigan, Iowa, Kentucky, Indiana and Washington all recognize a privilege to inform the employer. An Ohio case recognizes limitations on the methods of imparting such knowledge, where frequent telephone calls to the debtor at her place of employment were calculated to enlist the pressure of the curious and annoyed employer. Typical written communications in these cases speak "as one employer to another," "in the interest of a happier and more efficient employee," and "to spare you the inconvenience and expense of garnishment of wages," and the courts have found these not only to be inoffensive, but in fact a fair expression of the legitimate interests of the employer, and therefore privileged communication by the creditor.

Although this is clearly the prevailing view today, it would seem that the recognized policy of holding a creditor liable for shaming exposures is subverted. It is clear that the purpose is not to protect the employer, whatever justification that might afford, (and any employer who is interested can check the credit standing of his employee). Its object is to coerce payment from the employee by exposing him as financially unreliable to those persons upon whom his financial fortunes most depend. He will presumably make prompt amends to show it isn't so; or he will make timely payment in the first place, knowing such methods may be employed if he doesn't. The paternalism implicit in judicial opinions countenancing this practice, which belongs to another age, makes an employee's personal financial affairs the business of his employer.

An analogous injury to the employer would receive legal redress. If a creditor of the employer sent a communication to a person with whom the employer did business advising him of the employer's delinquency; soliciting cooperation in collection and warning that bothersome legal measures may have to be employed to secure money due the employer from the third person; and all this obviously to coerce payment, the court would have no trouble finding unjustified intrusion into legally protected relations. Equally clear

23

would be the wrong recognized if the employee received such a letter about his employer. There is no reason why employees should remain exposed to such injury.

Shadowing and Surveillance

Finding out things about a person, as well as telling them, may be an invasion of privacy. Police officers and private detectives occupy themselves with following, watching, and looking into things. There are limits within which these activities are free of legal liability.

If they are reasonable, these activities are allowed. Any proper police purpose pursued in a reasonable manner will justify police surveillance. Since the police act on behalf of the community, they are allowed somewhat greater latitude before their conduct will be characterized as unreasonable. Where there is harassment or intimidation, however, they are answerable for their conduct.

Private detectives or other private citizens who make the activities of others their business have some purpose. How reasonable it is will determine to some extent how much annoyance from it the law will condone. In this regard, publicity is given less weight than a legitimate private interest. A newspaperman who follows a person who is not in the public eye for a week to get material for a story on how that person occupies himself will have relatively poor standing against a claim of invasion of privacy. An investigator who follows an insurance claimant for a week to see how extensive alleged injuries really are will have much better standing. If the purpose is acquisition of newsworthy information, the policy of sacrificing privacy in the interest of public information will come into play.

A reasonable purpose must be served in a reasonable manner. If the insurance investigator makes himself conspicuous so that embarrassment or fright results, or does things which would make a normal person feel harassed, he can be called to account legally.

A few states have "peeping tom" statutes, which make looking in windows, doors, or other openings of a building for the purpose of "spying or invading privacy" a penal offense. No physical trespass is necessary. Generally, either by express terms of the law or judicial interpretation, police officers in the conduct of their duties are excepted.

In other states, persistent watching or following will be treated as a public nuisance when its effect is to annoy members of the general public or some particular portion of the public, and penal consequences may follow.

Computers, Data Banks and Dossiers

We come now to the increasingly insistent problem of man's ability to store data about people and its implications for individual privacy. The ramifications of computer-stored data reach into almost every aspect of modern American society. Record files accumulate from the moment of birth and absorb information about what an individual does or is for the rest of his life. School, employment, health, military service, financial data, arrest records, credit ratings are all grist for the memory mill. The compiling of dossiers about individuals' functions in both the public and the private sectors. The government maintains massive dossiers through military service records, social security, FBI and departmental files, to name only some of them.

This expansion of data gathering has been paralleled and perhaps even surpassed in the private sector. Business organizations and credit bureaus maintain extensive files of personal information which can be exchanged or purchased without the individual's knowledge that such a file even exists. Investigative organizations wield enormous power over the lives of individuals by storing information that can determine whether they will be hired, allowed to obtain passports, get mortgages or borrow money. Since these informational judgments inevitably become moral judgments, the right of a person to be sick or cantankerous or to have once committed a forgivable antisocial act becomes sharply circumscribed.

The proliferation of dossiers has become a matter of overwhelming concern to civil libertarians, legal scholars and many informed private citizens. Although there are unquestionable benefits accruing from this mass of data in terms

25

of organizational and technological efficiency, the concept of information gathering and retention does seem repugnant to the historic American notion of the rugged individualist whose freedom to be himself is his most cherished possession.

Credit Bureaus and Inspection Agencies

Outside of the federal government the largest information gathering systems are the credit bureaus. The credit bureau performs a necessary function in a highly fluid society such as ours and does enable prospective employers, merchants or mortgage lenders to make judgments based on factual information about people of whose personal life they know nothing. The problems arise not in the honest, factual information that is dispensed by the credit bureaus but in the publication of facts that may be irrelevant to the particular investigation, may be misleading or even erroneous. Violation of the right of privacy is at the heart of the question of how much information is known about a person and how freely it is circulated to people who have no legitimate interest in knowing everything in a given file.

Another investigative body that gathers and disseminates information about people's lives and habits as well as factual economic data is the inspection agency that delves into the backgrounds of applicants for insurance. This agency investigates very personal aspects of the applicant's life by talking to neighbors or associates, as well as gathering the factual material. In this way a great deal of subjective or openly biased information can find its way into a person's dossier. Since the investigators have neither the time nor the motivation to evaluate the material received, a good deal of conjecture and inaccuracy goes into the memory bank where it can remain for years. Thousands of people have been refused employment, credit or insurance because of derogatory information in their dossiers of which they are totally ignorant.

Fair Credit Reporting Act of 1971

Some of the concerns felt about unauthorized use of personal information, and the invasions of privacy represented by personal data files finally achieved a level of redress in the Fair Credit Reporting Act of 1970. Until that act was passed, the average citizen had no recourse against the agencies who compiled and disseminated information that may have been used against them. The credit bureaus are not accountable to anyone; the collection and sale of personal information is their business and they sell it to anyone who wants to pay for it. The citizen has no control over who has access to the information and no control over what kind of information is collected and retained.

There are various provisions in the act that seek to protect privacy to some degree.

1. The act requires that a report be requested only for a "legitimate business need" in regard to the report subject. It is not to be used by one individual against another for private purposes. Potential abuses of this provision seem very likely since an agency cannot spend the time and money checking out the absolute legitimacy of every request it gets.
2. When an investigative report is requested, the report subject must be notified. If the subject does not want the material in his file to be disseminated, he can decline to allow it to be given out although he will very likely not get whatever benefit he was seeking that activated the original request.

3. The act allows a person to know whatever information there is in the file about him except medical data and confidential sources of "personal information." However, an individual can enter into litigation to discover the sources if he wants to go to the trouble of doing so.

4. The user of a report is required to notify a consumer of the name and address of the reporting agency if the information results in an unfavorable decision against the consumer.

While this act does provide some protections and recourse for the report subject who feels that his privacy has been invaded and his prospects damaged, many of the provisions are unclear and offer sizable loopholes for the agency. The restrictions on the distribution of various kinds of information are not tight or precise enough to guarantee that information which may not even be wanted by the requesting party doesn't slip through.

The main benefits to be derived from the Fair Credit Reporting Act put the burden of proof on the consumer.

There are procedures that can be followed but they require effort and determination on the part of the individual who is attempting to safeguard his privacy. Obviously, it is extremely difficult and time consuming for any one person to combat the organized evasive skills of a large agency, but the remedies do exist and if one is willing to pursue a matter to its logical conclusion he may obtain the relief sought.

While no one seriously argues that credit and investigative agencies are not necessary features of American business and organizational life, the invasions of privacy caused by dossiers and data banks continue to grow as the technology becomes more efficient and hungrier for more information in more areas of life. Let us look at some of those other areas.

Arrest Records

Arrest records can provide a classic example of the balancing between the need of society to protect itself and the right of privacy of an individual who has been arrested but may have been arrested without probable cause, released without a conviction or finding, acquitted, or first convicted and subsequently acquitted.

These records are not only maintained by police departments and the FBI but also find their way into private, nongovernmental dossiers where there is little likelihood that the fact of an arrest, regardless of its eventual outcome, will ever be expunged. Thus the impact of an arrest, however misguided it may have been, can have a destructive effect on a person's later social and employment opportunities.

However, various states have in recent years enacted legislation requiring expungement of arrest records and/or return of photographs, fingerprints or other forms of identification. In the state of Washington an appeals court ruled that a defendant had a constitutional right within the penumbra of specific guarantees of the Bill of Rights to have her arrest record returned when the charges against her were dismissed. The state of Connecticut in 1974 enacted a bill that provided for the erasure of all court and police records if there was no conviction. In the District Court of the District of Columbia in 1974 the court held that in the case of *Menard* v. *Saxbe* that "when the FBI is apprised that a person has been exonerated after initial arrest, released without charge and a change of record to 'detention only', the FBI has the responsibility to expunge the incident from its criminal identification files."

Juvenile records are more likely to be sealed and considered nonexistent than adult records. This means in practice that after a charge has been dropped or successful probation completed, that the young person can truthfully claim that it never happened. Many states have not as yet decided to expunge or return arrest records in cases where there has been no conviction but the trend is moving in that direction.

The Direct Mail Industry

Among the purchasers of computerized personal information from whatever source they can get it are the direct mail companies. These organizations, heavily computerized themselves, manipulate millions of pieces of personal information about individuals and families to produce selective lists for sale to advertisers who have a product or service to sell and organizations that have a cause or philosophy to promote. While most people either simply discard unsolicited mail unopened and others scan it before throwing it out, enough people respond positively to direct mail solicitation to produce a profitable industry in terms of nationwide sales. There are some people, however, who find the receipt of unsolicited mail an incursion upon their personal privacy. The issue was often framed in terms of annoyance and dismay that information about oneself, often information that a citizen was obligated to furnish to satisfy a government requirement, was sold to business organizations for frank commercial gain. Sometimes the complaints centered on the nature of the material that was received into the household that may have been personally offensive. Other people felt that the simple fact that unwanted mail was being delivered to their homes was an invasion of privacy. A number of congressmen felt that the sale of government lists to commercial firms took unfair advantage of the private citizen. At this point, court challenges to the propriety of the sale of government lists to direct mail advertisers have failed to achieve any constitutional significance. There has also been some activity on the legislative level but no action has yet been taken.

Banks and Computerized Files

Banks are primary among the kinds of business organizations whose records and functions would be significantly improved by automating their operations. Most banks, even small ones, now have computerized records and can produce information about customers' transactions with much greater ease than in the more cumbersome manual days. Perhaps using this expanded record keeping capability as a starting point, the federal government in 1970 enacted into law the Bank Secrecy Act. The Treasury regulations, growing out of this act, required extensive record-keeping and reporting on the part of all banks. The putative reason for the Bank Secrecy Act was to supply federal agencies with information that would help them in "criminal, tax and regulatory investigations". There was particular emphasis on the foreign currency transactions in an effort to prevent large scale manipulations that deprive the United States government of large tax revenues. In theory the idea seems laudable; in practice, many bankers and other concerned people felt the provisions of the act and the implementing regulations were unconstitutional. The act required banks to keep microfilm records for two years of all checks in personal accounts, to keep records for five years of all non-real estate loans over $5,000 and all transfers of over $10,000. Reports of the designated transactions were to be made regularly to the Treasury Department. IRS agents, upon presentation of a subpoena, could gain access to customers' records without notification to the customer.

In a curious alliance of bankers and the California chapter of the American Civil Liberties Union, suit was brought against the Treasury Department to enjoin the Treasury regulations. The suit was brought on the grounds that the reporting provisions constituted a violation of Fourth Amendment rights against unreasonable search and seizure, and that there was too little control over the discretionary powers of the Secretary of the Treasury to request information. Another element of the suit centered on the formation of huge data banks that might become subject to abuse.

The reporting provisions for foreign transactions were not challenged. (*Stark* v. *Connolly*).

The Federal district court of Northern California ruled that the record-keeping requirements were constitutional but that the provisions of the act requiring reporting of domestic transactions were in violation of the Fourth Amendment protections against unreasonable search and seizure. The case was appealed to the Supreme Court (California Bankers *Association* v. *Shultz)* and all of its constitutional points were denied, even the matter of domestic reporting that had been upheld by the California court. The ACLU's contention that the record-keeping requirements violate its members' First Amendment rights by identifying its members and contributors was likewise denied by the majority opinion. The First Amendment guarantees to organizations like the ACLU the right to keep its sources of financial support anonymous. Under the record-keeping requirements, the government can easily get access to a list of ACLU contributors, which can in turn have a chilling effect on those supporters who choose to maintain an associational right of privacy. In the absence of any compelling state interest, many privacy advocates regard this decision as a regressive step in the struggle to enlarge the boundaries of constitutionally protected privacy.

Chapter 3
WRITTEN COMMUNICATION

Most communications considered so far were made to an indefinite group—the general public or some segment of it. They were made by means of books, magazines, newspapers, and broadcasts. In these instances (as well as those in which the communication was directed to some definite person) privacy was the concern of some third person who was neither the sender nor recipient, but rather the subject of the communication. In this chapter and the next, we are concerned with protection for the privacy of the parties to the communication.

MAIL

Private written communication is largely through mail and privacy is recognized and protected by federal law. There are, in addition, state laws designed to protect the privacy of written communications generally. However, laws which are intended for postal regulation are exclusively within federal jurisdiction, in accordance with the mandate of the Constitution that the Congress shall have power to establish post offices and post roads. Determining concretely the border between federal and state fields of jurisdiction—the point at which a letter is no longer postal matter—is something we consider shortly.

Protection Against What Is Exposed

There are laws to protect privacy of mail which restrict what may be exposed. This protects the privacy of the recipient from disclosures by the sender.

Federal criminal statutes place restrictions on what may appear on postal cards. It is an offense to write on a postal card any language of a threatening character or calculated and obviously intended to reflect on the character or conduct of another person. This would cover most subjects about which people are reticent. As an illustration that such reflection on character need not be of shocking proportions, a postcard message held to be a violation simply stated that a summons and complaint would be served at a certain time and place as previously arranged and no nonsense tolerated this time to avoid the service.

Another provision of federal law makes it an offense to send mail in envelopes or wrappers with delineations, epithets, terms, or language intended to reflect injuriously upon the character or conduct of another person. Besides constituting a punishable offense for the sender, the law forbids delivery by postal authorities and authorizes withdrawal of such items from the mail. In one case, colored envelopes were employed to coerce payment of money owed. The first dunning letter came in a pink envelope, the next in a black one with white lettering. The significance was generally known to post office employees. The court said that was enough; and that the color of the envelope was a "delineation" intended to reflect on the addressee's conduct in paying his bills. In another case, the very prominent appearance of "Excelsior Collection Agency" printed on the envelope and clearly not intended as a return address was held to violate this law, since the size and location served no legitimate postal purpose, and the sender's intention to coerce payment by the threat of this embarrassing reflection was apparent.

Protection Against Prying

Strong protection for privacy is given by a section of federal law, originally enacted in 1825, which makes it a crime to take mail before delivery to the addressee with design to obstruct correspondence, or *"to pry into the business or secrets of another,"* or to open, secrete, embezzle or destroy (italics added). The emphasized provision is of special concern here.

33

It is obvious, in the first place, that protection is afforded against snooping, whether motivated by malice or idle curiosity, even though the mail is not opened. The mail must, of course, be "taken." The law is not designed to punish snoopers whose intrusion is visual only. A "taking," however, need be no more than picking up a letter to examine it.

The intention to do a thing prohibited must be present at the time the mail is taken. If one accidently takes another person's mail, he incurs no liability for satisfying his curiosity by inspecting the envelope and perhaps even enjoying the scent of its contents, as long as the kiss that seals it is not violated.

Various circumstances have been considered under this law.

The fact that a letter had the business of the accused violator as its subject did not excuse him from the prohibitions of the law; nor did the fact that he himself wrote the letter. The fact that a letter is not sealed is immaterial. If the post office or mailman gives a letter to someone other than the addressee, that person has no better standing than he would have if he took the latter under other circumstances. If the sender of a letter retrives it from the post office, even after it is postmarked and consigned for delivery, there can be no violation of the law. But the sender has no right to take the letter once it is in process of delivery. The statute has been held not to apply to the taking of a letter addressed to a fictitious person, on the theory that provisions intended to secure privacy of communication have no application when such communication is impossible.

Mail Watch

The next section of the United States Code makes it an offense for any postmaster or other postal employee to unlawfully detain, delay, or open any mail.

This provision, in conjunction with the previous one, has been the basis of an attack on a post office practice known as the "mail watch."

Congress has given to the postal service, as to other agencies of government within its ultimate control, broad powers to regulate the conduct of its own business. Cooperating with other agencies of government, generally law enforcement, the Post Office has made available its services to watch all mail going to a designated address, noting the sender (from the return address), and perhaps other information, but limited to what appears on the envelope or wrapper. This limitation is imposed by the law forbidding opening of mail, and no postal regulation could lawfully defy or ignore this. Indeed, no act of Congress could change the law to permit such surveillance by opening mail, for the Constitutional guaranty of the people to be secure in their papers against unreasonable searches requires that a warrant for such search be obtained by any authority wishing to make it (see p. 87, *infra*). This Fourth Amendment protection has been determined by the Supreme Court to extend to mail.

The tax-evasion prosecution of Frank Costello was based in part on evidence obtained by a mail watch instituted at the request of the Internal Revenue Service, so the appellate court was told by Mr. Costello after his conviction. The court said that since only in unusual cases was mail delayed, and then for no more than one delivery, there were not unlawful delays violative of the statute, by postal employees.

Then turning to the provision making it a crime to take mail for the purpose of prying, the court said that the mail watch did not constitute a "taking" to pry into the business or secrets of another. Instead of adopting the position that superficial inspection and notation by postal authorities in the course of ordinary mail handling is not prohibited by the statute (even when for non-postal purposes), the court's opinion in effect sanctions a mail watch by anyone. With no qualification by express words or underlying reasoning the court stated ". . . without offense to Constitution or statute writing appearing on the outside of envelopes may be read and used."

Thus, apparently a new avenue of surveillance was opened to the great army of private and public investigators as well. Now a hotel clerk or apartment house employee who distributes mail can be used with impunity by those interested to note the identity of everyone sending mail to a particular person.

A moment's reflection will make it clear that hardly any area of one's life would remain private—what one reads where one banks or shops, to what organizations one belongs, what stocks one owns, one's doctor, lawyer, accountant. The list is only limited by the activities of a person's life.

The reluctance of the court to recognize a special privilege to pry available to postal employees is understandable, since the statute had been held previously to apply to such persons the same as to everyone else. Indeed, if there is to be protection against the evils of government surveillance it is important that this be so. It is hard to know what the court thought was the intended protection of the anti-prying provision. The court seems to hold that anything short of opening the mail would not be a violation. But if mail is opened, the anti-prying provision is superfluous, since the opening, by the terms of the statute, is itself as great an offense as prying.

It would seem that the solution lies in making a distinction between the "taking" of mail in a post office and the "taking" of it elsewhere. This is necessary if a very valuable protection for privacy is to be preserved.

Limits of Postal Protection

The Federal law extends to postal items only. It is obvious that at some point an item of mail is no longer in the postal system. At that point any protection will have to be based on state law, since under the Constitution matters of government not declared by the Constitution to be federal remain within the jurisdiction of the states.

A letter, when delivered to the addressee or someone authorized to receive it for the addressee, leaves the custody of the federal government and is no longer a postal matter. Any mail delivered into a mail receptacle until the addressee picks it up is still in the custody of the Post Office. Mail dropped through a mail slot onto the floor of a locked office has been held to be still within government custody, although mail placed on the addressee's desk has been held to be out of postal custody, and one who takes it does so free of the federal statute. One case holds that a letter was still in government custody when opened by someone who took it from the person to whose care it was addressed. The fact that the "care of" party was a general store on a small island, which served as a regular postal depository, probably accounts for this exception to the usual "care-of" rule. This rule is to treat such delivery as being to a person authorized to receive it for the addressee, and so the end of government custody.

TELEGRAPH

Telegraphic communication, although written communication, is largely protected by the same sort of laws that protect telephone communication. This is because both are wire transmissions and give rise to similar problems of protection.

Unlike the post, the telegraph is not exclusively within the jurisdiction of the federal government. The constitutional basis recognized for federal laws regulating telegraphic communication is the federal responsibility for regulating interstate commerce. The regulation of wire communication is shared with the states.

State Law

Laws enacted by the various state legislatures to regulate telegraphic communication within the state generally provide penalties for unauthorized interception of such communication by anyone. Other provisions forbid employees to disclose the contents, and are usually given effect to restrict any information about the communication or information derived from the message. Some states have anti-bribery provisions, making it unlawful to offer or accept a bribe calculated to induce disclosure. Other provisions prohibit the use of information unlawfully obtained. Some state statutes covering the subject provide against unauthorized opening of a telegram once the message has been reduced to writing and sealed in an envelope for delivery.

Federal Law

Federal laws protecting telegraphic communication derive mainly from the Federal Communications Act of 1934. By its terms it prohibits anyone involved in transmitting or receiving the communication from divulging or publishing anything having to do with it (including the very fact of its existence) outside the regular channels of communication. It makes an exception and permits disclosure in the case of demand by subpoena of a court, or proper demand by other lawful authority. It then prohibits *any* person from intercepting, divulging, or publishing anything having to do with the communication to anyone, unless authorized by the sender to do so. Further provision is made forbidding use by a person not entitled to it of information obtained by the receiver of the telegraphic transmission for the benefit of that person or anyone else; or any use by an interceptor or one who receives the information knowing it was intercepted. And any intercepted matter may not be divulged or published by anyone if it is known to be obtained by interception.

Giving these provisions their usual context of application, telegraph employees cannot divulge anything, except when subpoenaed or made subject to other legal process. They cannot use anything they learn for their own or anyone else's benefit.

No person—and this includes a police officer as well as anyone else—can intercept communications and divulge anything or use anything learned, without the authority of the sender. This restriction extends to anyone who knows of the communication and is aware that it is obtained by an interception.

The Supreme Court has interpreted the federal provision against divulging without authorization of the sender as applying to intrastate as well as interstate communications. This portion of the act speaks of "communications" without further qualification. The court, in giving sufficient latitude to permit application to local communication, simply adopts the view that the communications system itself is part of interstate commerce and that therefore its integrity is a proper subject for congressional legislation, regardless of the destination of a particular message.

GENERAL PROTECTIVE PROVISIONS

It is a feature of state penal legislation to make provision for protection of the privacy of written communications and other papers. Such provision is old in English common law, and the criminal liability of persons violating it was recognized by common law in this country before the enactment of penal statutes.

Typically there are two sorts of acts prohibited. One is the unauthorized opening of a letter or telegram or private paper that is sealed. The other is the unauthorized publishing of the contents of such paper or communication. Reading by itself, without any accompanying act that is forbidden, is not a crime. The law is sometimes written so that a person who reads a paper that is unlawfully exposed in his presence by someone else is liable. There is generally no prohibition against copying an already exposed paper if nothing else that is prohibited is done or intended.

There is some question about the extent of publication necessary for criminal liability. Is relating to one friend what one has read in a letter that lies exposed on a desk a criminal act? Or is more general publication necessary, to the public at large or to some segment of it? New York has decided, but without unanimity, to apply its law only when there is publication in the broader sense. This was chosen as an alternative to adopting the test of publication to even a single person, which satisfies the requirement of the law in the case of a defamation.

Chapter 4

SPOKEN COMMUNICATION

We turn now to privacy of the spoken word.

People are usually quite careful about what they write. It endures unless destroyed. What is spoken, however, leaves its trace only in the mind unless measures are taken to preserve it. In the world in which we live increasingly easy means are provided for this.

The telephone is a device designed to permit conversation at a distance, with the not surprising consequence that we cannot be sure exactly who is in the audience. Devices have been perfected to give admittance to unknown and un-wanted members. There exists in combination the un-guarded ways of ordinary speech, easy and undetected access to the conversation, and the means of preserving it. The temptation often proves too great for police and for private citizens who want to know about other people's business.

Further hidden threats to privacy are posed by the aston-ishing developments in the field of electronics which make possible undetectible eavesdropping at a distance. Here, unlike the case of telephone conversations, the speaker has not subjected his conversation to electronic channels of communication with the foreseeable risk that there may be unknown members of the audience listening and recording. The act of speech is itself perilous.

It is now not necessary that the eavesdropper be unseen, only that the eavesdropping be unkown. It is possible to elicit sought-after utterances to be preserved on recordings made by means of microphones and recorders now available in convenient sizes and disguises. One person having bugged himself or the place of the meeting, now has the means of creating a record of another's foolishness, induced for the purposes of the recording. On such recordings, serious designs to commit crimes or civil wrongs are indistinguishable from words which pass while a person toys with the idea of doing something wrong—a weakness which everyone indulges at times, and for which a person is called to answer only in a police state.

The bit of embalmed foolishness is usually vastly more persuasive than any later explanation of its innocent but embarrassing circumstances of origin. "The record speaks for itself," is the usual attitude, and only evidence that the recording is a fabrication or a distortion of what was actually *said* is given due consideration.

What does the law offer to protect privacy against such massive challenges?

TELEPHONE COMMUNICATION

Nature of Federal Protection

In the last chapter we had occasion to refer to the Federal Communications Act of 1934. The same section which relates to interference with telegraph communication is the basis of federal law restricting wiretapping of telephone communication. The same provision protects broadcasts against unauthorized interceptions, a matter of scant concern in a discussion of privacy and not taken up here. Since the communications system is interstate, federal law regulates all communication through it, even if intrastate.

Section 605 provides in part as follows:

"... no person not being authorized by the sender shall intercept any communication and divulge or publish the existence, contents, substance, purport, effect, or meaning of such intercepted communication to any person. ..."

This is the foundation upon which rests a considerable structure of case law consisting of numerous Supreme Court and other federal court decisions.

41

The acts prohibited by the Communications Act are crimes. This naturally affords a strong deterrent to illicit wiretapping practices by private citizens who would thereby expose themselves to criminal prosecution by federal law enforcement authority.

The prohibitions apply also to all law enforcement officials, both federal and state. When the law says "no person" it means no person, without implied exceptions for police or anyone else. Nothing short of an act of Congress can change this. No provision of a state constitution or state legislative enactment or judicial decision, nor any order of a Federal or state court can make lawful any acts that this law makes illegal. And law enforcement authorities, both state and federal, are in principle faced with the prescribed penalties of fine or imprisonment for violation.

This law has two edges: the sharper edge for preventing wiretapping by others than the police is the threat of criminal prosecution. Since such prosecution is discretionary with the prosecutor, it is not surprising to find something less than irrepressible enthusiasm when the prosecutor is asked to prosecute a dutiful, if overzealous, police officer or a member of his own staff. The other edge cuts better in such situations.

Three years after the enactment of the law the Supreme Court decided that evidence obtained by wiretapping interception of communication could not be introduced in federal courts. To allow such evidence into a trial would make the illegal act of divulgence a part of the legal proceeding. This would be an intolerable travesty, and any prosecution that depends upon such evidence must fail. Shortly thereafter, when the same case again came before the court it declared that evidence obtained as a result of leads gotten by wiretapping was also inadmissible, "the fruit of a poisonous tree." Thus the rule was developed that once there is a convincing showing to the trial judge that wiretapping was employed to obtain the leads, the prosecution has a burden of showing that its evidence is in fact of independent origin.

This doctrine must be viewed against the background of a legal policy to disregard the source of evidence or the manner in which it was obtained. It is true that some state and federal rules that place limitations of this sort on evidence do exist, but they represent departures from common-law tradition. It is also true that evidence obtained by violating a constitutional right is excluded. But this is because a conviction based on such evidence would be a denial of due process. Such a conviction, resulting in deprivation of life, liberty, or property, is nugatory by the terms of the Fifth and Fourteenth Amendments, which impose "due process" limitations on the federal and state governments respectively, and so on federal and state prosecutors.

Wiretapping has been held by the Supreme Court not to be a violation of a constitutional right. Hence the exclusion of evidence obtained by it is not required by the "due process" provisions. But the peculiar circumstance that *giving* such evidence and breaking federal law are one and the same act made its exclusion in the Federal courts almost inevitable.

Material illegally obtained by wiretapping may not be introduced as evidence in federal courts even when it was obtained by state agents completely without the knowledge of federal authorities. The Supreme Court decision to this effect was in a case in which the fact that the evidence was a product of intercepted communication came to the prosecutor's knowledge for the first time at the trial in federal court during cross-examination of a local police officer by the defense lawyer.

The Supreme Court has held that in a state prosecution evidence obtained by state agents in violation of the Communications Act may be used to obtain a conviction. The reasoning of the court was that the implied exclusionary intention of the act ought not to defeat the express words of the state legislature that authorized the admission of such evidence. The court said this would apply equally if the express authorization were by judicial decision of a state court. The court's position was that if Congress wishes to have such evidence excluded from state courts, regardless of state views, it must say so expressly.

Protection Against What

What, exactly does the act protect against? The judicial intepretations of two key words, "intercept" and "divulge," provide the answer. By the terms of the Act, an unlawful thing has been done only when a communication has been intercepted *and* divulged.

When is a communication intercepted? The Supreme Court has held that the use by government agents of a regular telephone extension with the consent of a party to the conversation, who was also the subscriber for the phone, was not an interception. The notion here seems to be that the telephone caller ought reasonably to expect that at the other end there is an extension which the other party may make available to someone else. Busy executives and their secretaries regularly use such an arrangement without notice to the other party, so there is no violation of customary standards of privacy in monitoring by extension. The court, in addition, placed emphasis on the literal meaning of interception as a taking physically located at a point *between* the parties, which extension monitoring is not.

The same physical criterion, this time applied at the originating end, was used by the court in deciding an earlier case. Here a device called a "detectophone" was used to listen to one party's part of a telephone conversation on the other side of a wall separating adjoining offices. This was eavesdropping on a telephone conversation, not interception, and the Court said the Communications Act provision did not apply. Analogy was drawn to a note containing a message to be telegraphed. Before it becomes telegraphic communication it is not a communication within the protection of this law, and taking it could not be an interception. If someone was in the room with the person on the phone and overheard his conversation he would not be intercepting a communication. The fact that it was overheard by someone in another room does not change the situation. The purpose of the act is to protect the means of communication, not to protect secrecy, said the court.

In between fall a variety of different techniques of gaining access to conversations and there are conflicting decisions in different federal courts in cases involving techniques that are indistinguishable. A geographical generalization is of small value, but it does seem that the federal judiciary on the West Coast has so far shown the most pronounced tendency to construe "intercept" narrowly and thus exclude from the range of the act's prohibition a larger number of wiretapping techniques.

Among those techniques whose harvest of evidence has been allowed is a tape recorder attached to a receiver; an induction coil at the receiving instrument; a "twinfon" device attached to a receiver, creating a temporary extension; a tape recorder attached at the bell-box; and even a line attached outside the house to the exterior telephone line to create an "extension." The last case relies on the Supreme Court decision allowing use of conventional extensions installed by the telephone company, but only to adopt the term "extension" as the criterion. If this case is followed, any technique which could be called an "extension" without doing violence to English usage will escape the prohibition against interception.

Other federal courts have given greater scope to the concept of interception, and found any technique that gives access to the message impulse at a point short of the ear of the person for whom it is intended to be an interception. Frequently a recording of a telephone conversation is made by one of the parties, rather than by a third person. It is a moot point whether such a recording is an interception, but the fact that a party rather than a third person taps in to record is irrelevant.

It is clear that pondering what is embraced by the term "intercept" is a sterile occupation. The real issue, as indicated by the Supreme Court on the occasions it has considered the matter, is what is the interest intended to be protected by the act. Once this is decided, the methods which pose a threat will be easily distinguished from those which do not.

The section of the law we are looking at forbids an intercepted communication to be divulged. What constitutes a divulgence?

The interception or its fruits may not be presented as evidence at a trial, and thus be divulged. But things other than this constitute the offense and are grounds for refusing the communication admission as evidence.

It has been held that any communication of what is intercepted by one officer to another in the course of their work is a divulgence, and that evidence obtained by the second man by using such material is tainted. When presented to a grand jury the intercepted communication is "divulged," and an indictment based on it is voidable, as would be the verdict of a trial jury.

Any communication from one person to another is a divulgence. The person intercepting need not even know the contents of the communication in order to "divulge" it. Thus a switchboard operator who cut into one line to give access to the call to persons on another line was held to be divulging an intercepted communication.

Who is Protected

The term "sender" seems to be a misnomer when referring to a party to a telephone conversation. It is a carryover from the predecessor legislation of Congress concerned with radio broadcasting and supplanted by the Federal Communications Act. Since it is the "sender" who must give authorization if interception and divulgence are to be innocent, it is important to determine who that person is.

There are decisions holding that *either* party to a telephone conversation is a "sender." There are others holding that the person speaking, with reference to any particular communication in the conversation, is the "sender." Still another view has been expressed that "sender" embraces *both* parties because the words of each form integral parts of the one telephone communication.

The view that either party is a "sender" results in finding authorization by either sufficient to legalize interception, while the view that both parties are "senders" entails authorization by both for legal interception.

Those cases which allow greater latitude for wiretapping, and which presently represent the prevailing opinion, favor the view that either party may be the "sender," so that one cooperating party may shield the police from the thrust of the statute. The apparent design of the law is frustrated by this interpretation, for it is clear that the purpose was not to provide privacy only for two persons who justify each other's confidence; but rather to provide privacy for any communication regardless of how trustworthy the recipient might prove to be. What the recipient does with what he hears is another matter, which is not germane to privacy of communication.

"Authorization" by the "sender" must be freely given. Thus when a person implicated was offered immunity from prosecution if she made certain telephone calls to another person which were to be recorded by the investigators as evidence, the court found that such acquiescence did not satisfy the requirement of "authorization." In another case, upon review by the Supreme Court it was held that confronting a party with transcripts of previously intercepted calls and thereby procuring consent to their use in evidence against another person did not constitute "authorization."

State Protection

The federal scene, unsettled as it may seem, is a model of clarity when compared to the situation in the states.

The field of regulation is one which federal and state law share and almost all states have statutes prohibiting wiretapping, or limiting the practitioners and the purposes for which it may be used. There are judicial decisions in the states passing on the evidence questions. The objectives of state law are the same as the federal, but with greater liberality generally in according powers to the police. The interests of police and prosecutor are generally more highly regarded in the states and their influence is strongly felt in the state legislatures.

A number of states have laws making wiretapping legal when done by certain persons, following certain procedures, and done for certain purposes. These statutes require orders of a court allowing taps by police and prosecutors, and provide that such orders, carefully circumscribed, be granted only when a probability of specific criminal activity is shown to the court. Evidence so obtained is admissible in state courts (see p. 43 *supra*) , and convictions will not be overturned.

There have been decisions in state courts, however, which refuse to issue an order permitting wiretapping in accordance with such a state law because the act it would authorize is illegal under federal law, the supreme law of the land. This, even though part of the supreme law of the land (a decision of the Supreme Court) does not require that evidence obtained by wiretapping be excluded from state prosecutions. And one opinion in a federal court of appeals case has questioned whether such a state scheme for legalized wiretapping is not really a design for systematic violation of federal law, rather than simply a state rule allowing the admission of evidence despite its source, which is all that the Supreme Court has countenanced.

EAVESDROPPING

Constitutional Protection

The problem of eavesdropping as it has developed under federal law is a constitutional question, rather than a statutory one. The portion of the Constitution invoked is the Fourth Amendment. It declares:

> "The right of the people to be secure in their persons, houses, papers, and effects, against unreasonable searches and seizures, shall not be violated, and no Warrants shall issue, but upon probable cause, supported by Oath or affirmation, and particularly describing the place to be searched, and the persons or things to be seized."

The paramount concern in this amendment is for rights of privacy. This has been made clear in cases arising from more obvious violations than eavesdropping (which are considered in Chapter VII). Formal acknowledgment of this is made in eavesdropping cases, but the rule adopted by the Supreme Court, and under constant fire from within the court, could hardly be less suited to achieve protection of privacy.

In the discussion of wiretapping *(supra, p. 44)* mention

48

was made of a case in which the facts included the use of a "detectophone," an instrument which was held against one side of a wall to hear amplified telephone conversation in a room on the other side. In addition to the rejected argument of telephone interception, it was contended before the court that such eavesdropping was an unreasonable search which violated the Fourth Amendment. The Supreme Court, in 1942, decided that it was not. Following a case decided fourteen years earlier (before passage of the Communications Act), which involved wiretapping in the basement of an office building, the court declared that unless there was physical intrusion into protected premises—the sort of physical intrusion which meets the technical requirements for a trespass—there could be no violation of Fourth Amendment guaranties.

Thus wiretapping is proscribed by the Communications Act more certainly, as an interception, if done off the premises than on; while eavesdropping must at least originate within the premises if Fourth Amendment protection is to be available.

Such physical intrusion, violative of the Fourth Amendment, was found by the Supreme Court in a 1961 case. Here a "spike mike" was introduced through the party-wall of two adjoining houses. The device had a spike, 11½ inches long, which picked up acoustical vibrations and transmitted them through an amplifier to a speaker or recorder. The probe through the wall and under a baseboard ended when a heating duct was reached. The duct system ran through the house, and voices in several rooms were clearly audible. Here, said the court, there had been an intrusion, rendering evidence obtained by it inadmissible. Speaking of the earlier case which first enunciated the physical intrusion rule that was reiterated here, the Court said "we decline to go beyond it, by even a fraction of an inch." Justice Douglas delivered a separate opinion:

"An electronic device on the outside wall of a house is a permissible invasion of privacy according to *Goldman v. United States* [the earlier case] while an electronic device that penetrates the wall, as

49

here, is not. Yet the invasion of privacy is as great
in one case as in the other. The concept of 'an unauthorized physical penetration into the premises,'
on which the present decision rests, seems to me to
be beside the point. Was not the wrong in both
cases done when the intimacies of the home were
tapped, recorded, or revealed? The electronic device—even the degree of its remoteness from the
inside of the house—is not the measure of the
injury."

The principle of physical intrusion has been tested in
instances where an agent or informer armed with hidden
recorder or transmitter enters the premises and engages the
suspect in conversation.

In the first case, the bugged person was an informer who
had the confidence of a suspected narcotics seller. The
Supreme Court upheld the admission of testimony given by
an agent waiting outside and listening to a receiver which
picked up the conversation sent by the informer's hidden
transmitter. There was a physical entry to be sure. But it
was consented to, hence no trespass.

The vitality of this decision has been greatly diminished
by subsequent ones. The major criticism centers about the
entrapment constituted by the suspect's ignorance of the
informer's true role. Can there be meaningful "consent"
under such circumstances? Only, it would seem, to the bare
act of physical entry. If the true role of the person bearing
the eavesdropping device is deemed significant, there was
no consent. The real trouble here again is in the court's
insistence on a simple test of physical trespass as the standard for constitutional protection.

This issue was taken up in a subsequent case involving
a hidden "minifon" tape recorder carried by an Internal
Revenue agent. Here, however, the agent identified himself
and stated the official purpose of his visit. The thing he
didn't tell was that he carried a recorder. Offers of bribes
were made by the taxpayer and preserved on tape. The
Supreme Court held the evidence admissible. The taxpayer
in this case had provided the evidence with knowledge that

50

he was disclosing something illegal to a government agent. In choosing to run this risk he surrendered his privacy—to the agent's mind and to a machine.

The dissenting opinion of Justice Brennan in this case is a powerful assault on those views which identify privacy with secrecy, and accord protection grudgingly only to secrets. "The right of privacy would mean little if it were limited to a person's solitary thoughts, and so fostered secretiveness. It must embrace a concept of the liberty of one's communications, and historically it has."

The issue was quite clearly defined. The majority considered the tape recorder as only a more reliable extension of the agent's memory. If it simply enhanced the credibility of his report it did not violate the rights and offend the interests protected by the Fourth Amendment. The minority stressed the facts of human sensibilities, and the inhibitory effect of surveillance and of preservation of what is intended to be transitory.

The "search" takes place somewhere. The physical intrusion test relates to that place. But can a physical intrusion into *any* place constitute a violation of the Fourth Amendment? The amendment speaks, in this connection, only of the right of the people to be secure in their "houses."

The words of the amendment are not construed to be a literal exhaustion of protected places, but rather a statement of the protection envisaged. Besides homes, such places as offices, stores, automobiles, hotel rooms, and even an occupied taxi are inviolable places. Any place from which one person has a right to exclude another, even though only temporarily, is a likely candidate for protection. The precise limits are not clear, but certainly one could not expect protection from eavesdropping intrusions in public places, at least not while they are freely accessible.

Evidence obtained in violation of the Fourth Amendment is inadmissible in federal courts. The reasons for its exclusion are twofold. One is that the alternative of allowing it in would leave the victim of illegal search and seizure as though the constitutional protection did not exist, and it is for the protection of persons in these precise circumstances that the constitutional guaranty exists. The other is that a verdict supported by such evidence would be a deprivation of life, liberty, or property without due process of law, and so denial of a right conferred by the Fifth Amendment.

This exclusionary rule for federal courts was laid down in a Supreme Court case decided in 1914. And in a case before the court in 1961 such evidence was ruled inadmissible in state prosecutions. This represented a sharp departure from previous decisions. It seems the court was much influenced by the failure of the states to do more themselves to frustrate the effect of police violations of Fourth Amendment guaranties which the Fourteenth Amendment obliges the states to abide by in their law enforcement activties.

It is important to make one thing clear before taking temporary leave of the Fourth Amendment.

It is fundamental that in no event are searches and seizures to be conducted for the purpose of obtaining evidence of guilt. That is to say, searches and seizures may not be authorized when their purpose is to obtain the means of convicting someone. Such a purpose is repugnant to the foundation of our political liberty and the jurisprudence which preserves it. It is the cornerstone of a police state and the legal system which serves it. The only proper purpose for searches and seizures is to obtain evidence of crime, when there is reasonable probability that a crime has been committed. What is seized may become evidence in a prosecution, but obtaining evidence for this purpose may never the purpose of the search. We are not open to being picked-over by police who have keen hunches, so that they may gather the means of convicting us. If they can demonstrate that their suspicions are likely ones, they can obtain a warrant to see if, indeed, a crime has been committed, and to take possession of what appears likely to be the products or instruments of the criminal acts. This limitation, though widely ignored in practice, is as basic as protection against involuntary self-incrimination to which it is close kin.

This point becomes important when considering how, if at all, electronic "searches" might be regulated by warrant.

Given the indiscriminate character of eavesdropping, how can a warrant specifying the objects to be "searched" for and "seized" by electronic listening be implemented with sufficient selectivity to prevent massive rummaging and accumulation of evidence of guilt? Upon a satisfactory answer depends preservation of Fourth Amendment rights in the age of electronics.

Statutory Protection

Eavesdropping has been recognized as a crime by the common law for centuries, and a number of states have provisions in their statutory law making it a crime.

Typically, what is prohibited is loitering about a building to overhear something for the purpose of disclosing it to annoy or harm someone. Sometimes electronic methods are expressly interdicted. Exceptions for law officers in the performance of their duties is usual, by express exception or implication. The threat of prosecution is an effective deterrent to the introduction of evidence obtained by eavesdropping in a civil suit. Such evidence is generally admissible in a criminal trial under the general policy of disregarding the source of evidence, provided, of course, that no constitutional right is violated (see p. 43 *supra*).

Chapter 5

PRIVILEGE TO WITHHOLD

There are occasions when we are put to inquiry under legal authority. It is necessary that a certain amount of privacy be sacrificed in the interest of resolving disputes in an orderly and reasonable way, and of affording security to the members of the community. But there are limits to inquiry, some imposed in the interest of privacy, some in the interest of fairness, or from other considerations of policy. It is those things privileged to remain undisclosed in the interest of privacy which we consider in this chapter.

A privilege not to disclose may be invoked because of the nature of the subject matter; or, in the case of a communication, because of a special relation between the parties to the communication.

These privileges are not all given general recognition. Some are recognized in all the states and have a venerable history of descent in the English common law. Others are recognized in only one or two states.

A privilege may be grounded in the common law of a state. A large number have their bases in statutory enactments, or even rules of judicial procedure authorized by state or **federal** statute. Or the privilege may derive from state or **federal** constitutional provisions.

The chief occasion for the exercise of the privilege is, of course, when giving evidence as a witness in court; but some other legal proceeding at which a person is examined may be an appropriate occasion.

PRIVILEGED SUBJECTS

Certain subjects are privileged because their disclosure would result in an unjustified injury to privacy.

Trade secrets include a variety of confidential items of importance to a business. The owner may claim a privilege to withhold such matters as long as fraud in the administration of justice does not result. It is up to the judge to determine what is a trade secret, and to determine when refusal to disclose it is unjustified because of the unjust consequences.

Theological opinions or religious beliefs are privileged, so that every person has a right to refuse to disclose *his* as long as they are not a material issue in the action. (The issue of a witness' credibility does not involve the question of his religious beliefs, and therefore will not justify insistence that he disclose his beliefs.)

A right to withhold information about political opinions, activities, or associations has recently been recognized by the Supreme Court. It is rooted in the First Amendment guaranty of free speech and liberty of political action. It is therefore applicable in federal proceedings, and in state proceedings by virtue of the Fourteenth Amendment. Since the authority for this privilege is the Bill of Rights, the privilege exists in all governmental proceedings, rather than being limited only to those proceedings which are under the aegis of a court.

This privilege is much qualified by certain interests of government, particularly in security, and the limits of its recognition are not at all clear yet. The main thrust is protection of refusal to reveal political matters when no proper governmental purpose which the information would serve is apparent in the proceeding.

In most decisions recognizing this right, the proceedings under consideration sought information about the political activities and associations of others as well as the one claiming the privilege. It is not yet clear whether the privilege could be asserted by those whose politics are the subject of the disclosure when the disclosure is sought from someone else.

Privacy of the ultimate political act of a citizen—his vote —is protected. A privilege is recognized to keep undisclosed the tenor of the vote, unless it is found that the vote was cast illegally. The privilege belongs to the voter. An early case suggested that this privilege be available to exclude another person's testimony as well. This suggestion is obviously of significance only when the secrecy of the ballot has been violated.

A limited privilege to withhold facts which are matters of personal disgrace or infamy to a witness is available to him. The privilege cannot be invoked by him to avoid impeachment of his credibility.

Highly embarrassing things are not enough. Distinctions defining the privilege have traditionally been drawn between avoiding disclosure of what is in fact a disgrace or an infamy; and being obliged to disclose something which merely tends to disgrace a person or make him infamous.

Probably the best known of all privileges to withhold is the one excusing a person from telling anything which may incriminate him. It is expressed in the Fifth Amendment by the words "nor shall [any person] be compelled in any criminal case to be a witness against himself." When given direct, literal application, this is not protection of privacy. Rather, it is protection against coercion (in its varying degrees of brutality), and protection of a fundamental concept of fairness which shrinks from the power to compel conviction from the mouth of the accused.

The privilege against self-incrimination is available, however, to persons other than those accused of a crime. Thus, when a person is reluctant to give evidence in a civil proceeding or make disclosures before a legislative body because the facts sought may be a basis for future criminal prosecution, he may refuse; and the same privilege exists where he is called merely as a witness in a criminal prosecution. Not because it is unfair to force a man to convict himself by his own words, but because there is a privilege to hold back things which may later have the dire consequences of criminal punishment. Such things may be kept private with impunity.

PRIVILEGED COMMUNICATIONS

General Principles

America's great scholar of the law of evidence, John Henry Wigmore, has distinguished four basic conditions for the establishment of a privilege to refuse disclosure of communications.

The communication must originate in a confidence that disclosure will not be made.

This element of confidence must be essential to maintaining a satisfactory relation between the parties.

The relation of the parties must be one which the community thinks ought to be promoted.

The injury to the relation resulting from the disclosure would be greater than the benefit of getting at the truth resulting from the evidence disclosed.

These are abstract principles arrived at by analysis of the privileges which are recognized and the considerations that brought them into being. They show the shape of the interest in privacy which the privileges are designed to protect.

Once a privilege is recognized it is respected and carries the force of law, and no justification need be offered each time it is invoked. It is automatically available when the evidence offered is shown to be a communication of the sort which a privilege covers. Conversely, simply showing that a particular communication is confidential in all respects and meets all the standards underlying those privileges which are recognized will not avail to exclude the communication. It must be shown to be between parties who are in a relation for which the law provides a privilege.

There is understandable reluctance to extend such privilege because room for getting at the facts is cut down. And without facts, justice cannot be done.

Accountant and Client

Among the privileges most recently accorded by the legislatures of various states is one for communication between accountant and client, now recognized in at least thirteen states. The form of the statute may be to restrict examination of accountants, or to restrict testimony about communications; and some provisions require the client's consent, rather than simply giving a client the privilege to object. The privilege is the client's, since he is the one to be protected.

Journalist and Informant

Journalists are another class lately given consideration. At least twelve states have laws protecting against disclosure of sources of information. About half expressly include radio or television within their protection. It should be noted, however, that only one state, Michigan, has a law conferring a privilege for the *communication* between reporter and informant. All the others merely privilege a refusal to disclose the *source* of the information, and so are not really based on a recogniton of a confidence to be kept private—indeed, publication is the very purpose of the communication—but rather upon recognition of something private to be protected, something which is part of the professional resources of the journalist. The underlying policy of protection is akin to that of trade secrets (see *supra,* p. 55).

The privilege is the journalist's, not the informant's, and like all privileges may be waived by the one who may invoke it. This leads to a result uniquely paradoxical among professional communications. The person whose confidence is to be respected—the informant—receives protection only derivatively from the journalist's privilege to refuse disclosure. No independent privilege is available to the informant to keep his identity private, and the journalist would be free to disclose it if, for instance, he no longer had an interest in the informant as a future source. The one who is directly protected—the journalist—has reposed no confidence. He is interested only in keping undisclosed a valuable asset, not in protecting a confidence.

The customary argument for a journalist's privilege—to safeguard freedom of the press—must be weighed with this in mind. Also to be considered is the plight of a person harmed by the publication of a story who cannot air pertinent facts in court because the source is privileged.

Clinical Psychologist and Client

Ten states confer a privilege protecting communications between client and clinical psychologist. This is quite apart from the privilege for psychiatrist-patient communications, which is covered by the physician-patient privilege in those states in which it exists. It is an interesting anomaly that four of the ten states protecting clients of psychologists have no statute conferring a general physician-patient privilege, leaving psychiatrists and their patients in a moot position.

Attorney and Client

Of the generally recognized privileges to withhold communications, the attorney-client is the oldest and most firmly established in policy. Though statements of the privilege vary somewhat in different states, it is everywhere a privilege belonging to a client who has formed a lawyer-client relationship with a lawyer. It permits him to refuse to disclose, and to prevent the lawyer from disclosing, all communications made in confidence for the purposes served by the relationship. It can be waived only by the client.

If the communication becomes known to a third person while being made, such third person may disclose it. It is up to the client to insure the security of his communications. If it is disclosed to someone else by the lawyer in breach of his duty of confidence, however, its exclusion may be insisted on.

If the client has consulted a lawyer for the purpose of committing a crime or a civil wrong, communications are not privileged. If the issue in dispute is between lawyer and client, the privilege does not apply to relevant facts. When several persons are represented by the same lawyer and later became adversaries in a law suit, what the lawyer said when he represented them all is admissible if relevant.

Various exceptions are made where the policy of the rule would not be served by literal application—for instance, where the lawyer is a witness to the signing of a document and communications concerning its execution are relevant in later litigation.

The privilege extends to communications which are made to, or come to the knowledge of, stenographers, clerks, and other employees of an attorney.

The attorney-client relationship must exist. But it need not be formally established, and seeking advice casually would be enough if the intention were consultation of a lawyer in his professional capacity.

All attorney-client relations are not confidential, and so all communications are not privileged. The presence of a third person who is not there for the purposes of the attorney-client meeting destroys the privacy necessary for a confidential communication. This means, for instance, that at conferences and closings at which clients and their attorneys meet with others to transact business what is said openly between attorney and client is not privileged.

While the contents of legal papers are normally privileged communication, the acts of executing or witnessing them are not. An exception is sometimes recognized in the case of a will, where the client's interest in keeping confidential the fact that he has made a will confers privilege regarding the act of execution. But this privilege lasts only during the lifetime of the client.

It is important to note that the privilege belongs to a client even though he has no involvement in the proceeding in which disclosure is sought. He may exercise it to prevent disclosure of matters of communication between him and his attorney in any action, whether or not he is a party. And a party to an action who is not the client with reference to a communication, cannot invoke the privilege to keep it out of evidence.

Husband and Wife

It is a matter of common acceptance that the least surrender of privacy by communication takes place in communication between husband and wife. It is natural that the law should confer a privilege for such communication.

The parties must be man and wife, living together at the

time of the communication, in order to enjoy the privilege. Communications between separated persons are not privileged. This is reasonable enough, since there no longer exists bounds of privacy surrounding their lives as man and wife.

It is presumed than an intention to keep such communications private existed when they were made, but circumstances indicating that this was not the case result in a loss of the privilege. When a third person is present or when transmission to a third person is intended, the words are not confided, and so are not protected. Some state statutes omit the qualification that the privileged communication be confidential and the courts read the text literally with the result that in several states any communication between husband and wife is privileged. This seems not to serve the purpose of the privilege, and results in unjustifiable exclusions of evidence.

Some state laws extend the privilege beyond communications to whatever facts are learned in the marital relation. The rationale is that the privacy which the privilege is intended to secure extends to noncommunicative acts as well as communications, and so should the protection. This is clearly sound in those cases where acts are a substitute for communication; or where the acts are done relying on the privacy of the marital relation. But it is unsound where the acts are done surreptitiously and observed by the spouse who is in fact being excluded from the marital confidence.

Paralleling the attorney-client privilege, the privilege is denied where the communications are germane to an action by one spouse against the other. Also similar is the limitation of the privilege so that a third person who overhears may testify to what he heard.

The privilege belongs to the person—husband or wife— who has made the communication. Although the other spouse cannot object to admission into evidence of what he or she merely has heard, an objection can be raised to testimony that he or she was silent in reply to something, since such silence is construed to be a communication.

The privilege does not terminate with the death of the

person communicating, nor with divorce. If the rule were otherwise the benefit of such privacy—confidence in the marriage—would be undermined by the fear of disclosure in the uncertain future.

Doctor and Patient

In England, a physician-patient privilege has been considered and rejected. In the United States, New York was the first state to enact such a privilege, in 1828, and at the present time the privilege is part of the laws of about two-thirds of the states.

A substantial body of legislation directed to other ends has curtailed the privilege in special instances. These include testimony in workmen's compensation actions, and testimony dealing with health and criminal problems, such as venereal disease, narcotics addiction, and gunshot wounds. In these matters a doctor's testimony is essential to effectuate the objectives of the law, and the privilege to withhold is abridged.

Like other relations, communication between physician and patient must be confidential in its origin to be privileged. This is generally presumed from the nature of the relationship, but it may be shown not to be so by the particular circumstances.

The privilege is not construed to extend to communications to dentists, veterinary doctors, or nurses working independent of a doctor's supervision. But a nurse or anyone else who is working under the control of a physician is a party with whom communication is privileged.

When consultation without treatment is the occasion for communication, the physician must be consulted in his professional capacity for the consultation to be privileged. Again as with the attorney, there are borderline cases which cannot be determined by general principles of application, but only by getting the drift of the particular facts.

A relation of physician and patient must exist. This results in a denial of the privilege when the physician retained by one side in a suit examines the opposite party for purposes of testifying as an expert witness about that party's condition.

Entries on medical records, including hospital records, are within the privilege.

The privilege extends only to communications *necessary* to achieving the benefits of medical care, by the terms of most state laws. But the communication may be an exhibition, inspection, or procedure, as well as written or spoken words.

Only the substance of the communication is privileged, not the fact that a person called or visited a doctor, or any circumstances of time, place, or identity in connection with the call or visit.

In several states the privilege exists only in civil cases, but in most it is available in either civil or criminal.

The privilege may not be invoked by a patient to exclude relevant evidence in a medical malpractice suit, thereby depriving the doctor of his defense.

The patient, and not the physician, is the one entitled to the protection of the privilege. Any patient, not just one who is a party to the action, is entitled to invoke the privilege with regard to communications with his physician. But a party to an action who is not the patient cannot invoke the privilege.

To assure present peace of mind of the one protected, the privilege survives the death of the patient.

When a waiver has been made at a former trial, privacy is gone, and testimony of communications is admitted at a subsequent one. When a physician is called by a patient to testify as a witness, there is a waiver of privilege for all matters raised. The patient's attorney cannot, in effect, use the privilege as a censoring device upon cross-examination to produce only testimony which he wants. The waiver extends to all testimony about the same medical conditions from other physicians or medical sources.

Religious Confessions and Communications

In more than two-thirds of the American jurisdictions a privilege covering confession to a priest is recognized. The statement of the privilege makes it a suitable protection for the traditional Roman Catholic confessional, but its scope extends to any religious confession made to a minister of any religion in the course of religious practice. Some statutes extend the privilege to communications made by any person "professing religious faith, or seeking spiritual guidance" (Georgia), or "any confidential communication properly entrusted to him in his professional capacity" (Iowa). These provisions place emphasis on the privacy of disclosure, which protects the interest of the person speaking to his religious counselor.

The traditional protection of the confessional is rooted historically in the secrecy of confession which is, according to religious precepts, to be preserved inviolate. The law determined to respect these precepts. Thus the privilege is at least as much directed to avoid conflict with religious practice as to preserve the confidences of the penitent. It would seem both from the logic of this policy and the wording of statutory provisions that priest or penitent may invoke the privilege in the first instance. Where the privilege is waived by the penitent, however, it would not be available to the priest. Certainly this would be the case in those states (of which there are fourteen) whose statutes deny the privilege when the penitent's consent is given. Laws in several states abrogate the privilege if the penitent testifies at all about the confession himself, which is again a shift of emphasis away from protecting the seal of the confessional in the interest of religion, and toward protecting the confidential character of the penitent's confession as long as he respects it himself.

Chapter 6

CONFIDENTIAL INFORMATION

There is great value in information. Occasionally information may be made freely available without consequent loss of value to its previous possessor. When this is so it is usually because the information had little value in the first place. Normally the worth of information depends upon limiting its circulation.

We are concerned now with protection of information which is one man's business and which he intends to keep private by limiting its currency within the bounds of confidence. It is not the problem of protecting proprietary interests in information of value with which we are concerned. That is a matter of property protection. It is preserving the bounds of confidence and limiting circulation of certain things within these bounds that is the keystone of privacy in this area, and the subject of this chapter.

TRADE SECRETS

What Qualifies

The term "trade secret" is one of convenience in legal parlance, and includes innumerable varieties of items of business information. Some are true secrets, known only to an intentionally restricted group. Other sorts   trade secrets may be acquired by anyone who applies himself, though often not without considerable expenditure of effort, time, and money. Protection is not limited to those situations in which the information is truly secret. The policy was expressed by Justice Holmes: "The plaintiff has the right to keep the work it has done, or paid for doing, to itself. The fact that others might do similar work, if they might, does not authorize them to steal the plaintiff's." The right recognized for either sort of trade secret is that of keeping private a matter whose business value depends upon its being kept within the business.

Among the things enjoying status as trade secrets are formulas, manufacturing processes, machinery, designs, methods of accomplishing various things, blueprints, sources of supply, marketing data, lists of customers. In fact, any information may become a trade secret if it is of value in a business, is confidential, and is of continuing usefulness.

Information is different than personal skills or abilities, which cannot be trade secrets. When an employee perfects skills and learns how to do certain work well his skill does not become something which a business may protect as a trade secret. This applies, of course, to all personal abilities involved in the enterprise, individually and collectively.

To receive recognition as a trade secret, a thing must have importance in the business which makes it worth protecting. Bare insistence that a thing remain unknown to others is not enough.

Information which relates only to a single occurrence in the life of the business cannot be a trade secret. Thus, for example, the amount of a bid submitted, or the time when an important announcement is to be made cannot be a trade secret though it is information of the greatest importance and of a highly confidential nature. Protection for such information is discussed later in this chapter *(infra,*p. 72) Trade secrets are parts of the business itself, not isolated matters in the course of its conduct.

A trade secret belongs to a particular business, not to a trade or industry. When things are matters of knowledge in the trade generally they can no longer be trade secrets. This does not mean that knowledge in the trade of the fact that one company has a special process deprives that company of trade secret status for its process. It is general familiarity with the process itself which would make the difference.

A thing which is made known to the public, such as the ingredients of a product recited on its label, loses whatever protection it might have as a trade secret by virtue of the general disclosure.

The most important qualification is that the information be confidential. The simple fact that something is not known doesn't mean that it may not be learned by inquiry or inspection and then used or disclosed to others. Only when the circumstances or an expressed intention make it clear that information is to remain private is such information limited to the persons and purposes to whom and for which willing disclosure is made.

Role of Patent and Copyright

Patent and copyright laws are of interest in connection with trade secrets.

While a trade secret may be the sort of thing entitled to patent or copyright protection—a new device invented in the shop, or a booklet setting forth methods of market analysis—it is often unwise to obtain such protection. Registration for patent or copyright protection means making the thing available to public inspection. Whatever value a trade secret has by virtue of being unknown would be lost. It is usually the idea or content (which cannot be protected by copyright or patent), not its protectable expression or embodiment, which makes a trade secret valuable. Protection against copying or duplication of a particular design or presentation may be valueless. And disclosure to the world of the underlying idea, which is the price of such protection, diminishes its value to the business.

As it happens, most trade secrets are ineligible for copyright or patent protection to begin with. Either they do not exist in a form which can be the subject of such protection or they lack the requisite originality or novelty. Things which are trade secrets but not patentable include old inventions put to new uses; substitution of one element for another, the substitution typically offering some advantage in cost or availability; or just the discovery of some "scientific principle."

It may be noted in passing that mere application for a patent, with the necessary disclosures limited to the patent office, does not result in the loss of trade secret protection. Even when two applications are made covering the same things, an adjudication of this interference by the patent office does not result in loss of trade secrecy since both applicants are presumed to have the knowledge already.

Protection Against What

The protection is against others acquiring trade secrets by improper means, or through violation of a confidence in which it was disclosed. The protection extends to situations where the information is acquired by mistake.

If the information is of the sort which would be available only by authorization for some purpose limited by the authorization—such as disclosure to employees who need it to do their work—the law affords protection against acquisition by someone not authorized to have it. Outright theft, clandestine copying or observation, or memorizing, are all ways of improperly acquiring trade secrets without a breach of confidence.

The more typical situation involves things disclosed in confidence, or things acquired by an employee in the course of his employment which the employer is interested in keeping confidential.

If one person opens another's mail by mistake and is apprised of a trade secret his innocence in coming upon it does not relieve him from respecting the confidential nature of what he has learned. Use or disclosure will entail liability. There must be facts present, however, which reasonably indicate to the recipient that the information is confidential.

If the person who acquires the trade secret of another discloses it, protection may be available against use or further disclosure by the one to whom it is related. This protection depends on whether the recipient of the information knew, or ought to have known, that the information was acquired by improper means or was disclosed in violation of a trust. If so, he is equally liable. If not, he has no liability to the owner of the trade secret until he has notice of the true situation. Even then he will not be liable if, in all innocence, he has paid for the information or has committed himself to a venture based on the information and it would now be unfair to deprive him of its benefit.

Excluded Persons

What sort of confidential relations or situations give rise to the trade secret problem?

The majority of cases involve employees and concern their conduct during and after their employment. The issues raised in this regard are considered in the next section.

Besides regular employees various sorts of agents—such as sales representatives—acquire knowledge of trade secrets in the course of the work they do for firms employing them. They are bound because of their relation not to use or disclose these confidential things, whether or not provision is expressly made in the agreement under which they work. In the absence of such provision there is, however, more room to question the confidential character of things disclosed to them.

Someone not in any sense in the regular employ of a business may be given a job to do—an electrical contractor, for instance, employed to rewire certain machines that perform operations which constitute a trade secret. In this instance the relationship is not naturally a confidential one, nor do the circumstances in themselves place a seal of confidence on what is learned in the course of the work. The manufacturer must ask that such matters be treated as confidential by the contractor and gain his assent, if there is to be a legal basis for protection of the trade secret. The request and the consent may be implied, as in a case where notices are posted making nondisclosure a condition of entering a restricted area.

Prospective purchasers of a product or a business, or prospective representatives or suppliers, present a thorny problem of confidence. To give consideration to the business opportunity at hand, it is necessary for them to find out things which are trade secrets. But not yet having entered into fixed business relations with the owner, they are dealing entirely at arms length. A blanket resrtiction on all that is learned, if the transaction does not take place, is normally not fair. It would tend to cut off independent development along the same lines for fear of a lawsuit claiming piracy of trade secrets uncovered at the time of the previous negotiations. However, the courts do tend to give protection when the outside party makes the initial overtures to find out trade secrets, or when it seems clear that secrecy was intended to be preserved and this was understood.

Employees

Employees present a special problem. The interest of the employer in keeping his business to himself must be balanced against the employee's interest in getting ahead by use of his experience, either in his own business or working for someone else. The difficulties arise when what an employee knows is used to his or someone else's advantage and to the disadvantage of his employer, usually now his former employer.

An employee may do what he likes with his skills. The fact that they were perfected or acquired at a particular place of employment gives the employer no right to restrict their use after the employment ends. But this does not mean that trade secrets developed by the skill of an employee may be used by him elsewhere, even when they could have been independently developed by the exercise of his talents. The law does not respect the potentialities of ubiquitous genius at the expense of the accomplished facts of a business which made the expenditures and took the risks necessary for the accomplishment.

Perhaps the element which weighs most heavily in deciding these cases is betrayal of trust. Information must be confidential to be a trade secret. The employee is here admitted to his employer's confidence for the purposes of the work he is to do, and nothing more. If the employee uses, or prepares to use, confidential material for other purposes while still employed he is betraying a trust. If, however, he waits until after he leaves and then uses what he has learned, with no previous deliberate scheme pursued to this end, the equities of the situation are different. It is still a breach of confidence, but under circumstances in which the employee's interest will receive more favorable consideration in the balance because of the absence of a *betrayal* of trust.

Those cases in which the employee betrays the confidence of his employer for the advantage of the employer's competitor weigh most heavily against the employee, presumably because the employee's interests have the least relative merit in such a case. He is not advancing himself, but simply profiting from things entrusted to him by violating the trust.

No single thing is more important to a business enterprise than its customers. It is not surprising that the trade secret most frequently in litigation is a customer list.

When an employee is furnished with a confidential list by his employer, the item is a protectible trade secret. When the list is a compilation of prospects which could be duplicated without much trouble by anyone, it is not a trade secret. The confidential list has value because it identifies ascertained sources of profit. When the information is exploited by others its value is diverted to their benefit. If the confidential list is the result of time and effort spent by the employee on behalf of his employer, the information belongs to the employer after the employee leaves. It is on this point that the most difficult disputes arise.

Frequently the trade secret controversy is given its impetus by the employer's desire to prevent a former employee from competing with him, which means trying to do business with the same customers. A court will not enjoin this competition unless it is shown that foul play by the employee is its basis. Solicitations based on remembering the employer's customers and what is likely to win their business is not a legal wrong, even if such information also had been compiled in confidential lists and records. If the employer wants to protect himself against such contingencies he may provide in an employment contract for restrictions against employee competition after the employment. Otherwise he is not entitled to such restrictions. Where, however, there is a pattern of systematic exploitation of confidential customer data, courts often discern an unfair practice. This is especially true when, as is frequently the case, preparation for these competitive activities were made before the employment ended.

Remedies

When the facts presented are found to constitute a violation of trade secrecy entitled to protection remedies are tailored to fit the harm done or threatened.

The court may enjoin the use of the information, or the sale of the product resulting from its use. It may enjoin further disclosure, or order an accounting and payment of profits resulting from the illicit use. When an entire business is based on another's trade secrets, further conduct of the business may be enjoined. If none of these remedies compensates for the harm already done, damages may be collected for particular injuries to a business resulting from loss of trade secrecy.

CONFIDENTIAL BUSINESS FACTS

One of the features of a trade secret is its continuing usefulness in a business. But information relating only to an isolated business matter which is confidential may be protected against rival use. Legal liabilty exists where a *rival* business interest procures by improper means information about business investments or price quotations, for example, which are confidential and whose possession, use, or disclosure by another causes harm.

A rival business need not be one in direct competition. Any adversity of business interest imports this protection. Opposite parties in business negotiations are "rivals." A supplier to a business is a "rival" of the competitors of that business, since the supplier stands to gain from its own customer's competitive success.

Improper means of acquiring such information exist in

the same instances where impropriety would be found in the case of a trade secret (see p. 68 *supra*).

In order for information to be considered confidential, it cannot be freely given to parties who make inquiry. Thus business information made available to credit agencies or trade associations is no longer confidential.

ENTRUSTED INFORMATION

Information which is given in confidence outside of business relations may be entitled to legal protection. The key is the relation between the one who imparts and the one who receives. The relation must be fiduciary, which is to say no more than that the information is entrusted to the recipient to be used for the benefit of the one giving it. This trust cannot be violated without legal consequences.

A fiduciary relation may subsist in many casual contacts. It is expected that fiduciary duties bind an attorney or a trustee or a banker in their respective capacities. But it also extends to a real estate broker who receives information about property in connection with an application for a mortgage loan; or a surveyor hired to survey property, with regard to information affecting a prospective purchase. There are two questions which should be asked to determine whether a fiduciary relation exists. Is the information being *entrusted* for some purpose? Is that purpose something done on behalf of the person entrusting it? If both answers are affirmative, there is the makings of a fiduciary duty with regard to the information.

The duty of the fiduciary is not to use the information for his own account in competition with the person giving it to him, or in any way which will cause the informant injury. The information may even not be related to the transaction at hand, but this duty still prevents use of it unless it is a matter of general knowledge, in which case it is not the sort of thing which may be made the subject of a confidence in the first place. The duty to keep the trust continues after the termination of the relation which gave rise to it.

If some further person receives the information knowing it is disclosed in breach of a fiduciary duty, he is also bound.

Only if he had no reason to suspect what the true source is, and doesn't find out until he has involved himself, is he free from liability. If the fiduciary's disclosure has resulted in the information becoming a matter of general knowledge, there is no longer anything which is a subject of protection, and anyone may avail himself of the information without liability.

The improper use or disclosure of such confidential information imposes liability for all gains resulting from the use or disclosure, and is subject to appropriate restraints by the court.

Protected information includes that which is *acquired* on behalf of another to whom the one acquiring it owes a fiduciary duty. Such information becomes a subject of trust, the same as information furnished in confidence.

CONFIDENTIAL DISCLOSURES TO GOVERNMENT

Departments and agencies at all levels of government have become vast repositories of confidential information. In according these organs of government the right to require such information, legislative bodies have exhibited a high degree of care in providing against improper use or disclosure.

Federal law provides that census information may not be used except for the statistical purposes for which it is supplied; that sources of information may not be publicly identified; and that copies of reports retained by individuals are immune from all legal process.

Income tax return information is protected by federal law against any disclosure except as authorized by law. Such authorization is extremely narrow, for the most part limited to tax collection purposes. But unlike census reports, retained copies of income tax returns may be required from the taxpayer by legal process.

A blanket provision of federal law makes it an offense for any federal official or employee to disclose any confidential information acquired in the course of his duties, except as authorized by law. This extends to the contents of all returns and reports.

Chapter 7
RIGHT TO BE SECURE

Privacy cannot exist at all without protection from bare physical intrusion. If private things cannot be secure in private places, all measures to provide safeguards for their communication or disclosure are pointless. If people cannot insist on the inviolability of their physical persons and cannot live part of their lives in places where the scrutiny of public authority is shut out, the concept of privacy of human personality is an empty one.

Making privacy secure is one interest. Making lives, property, and other things of importance in the community secure is another interest. The right of physical exclusion cannot be absolute when the security of the community requires an intrusion. But curtailment of the right of exclusion must be reasonable.

The protection against unreasonable searches and seizures afforded by the Fourth Amendment (p. 48 *supra*) was discussed in connection with eavesdropping, in Chapter 4 . What is said in a protected place is a thing protected. But the amendment's protection of privacy extends to more than places, and to more than words in those places.

At the time of its origin the authors of the amendment had in mind recent events of colonial rule, during which time general warrants and writs of assistance were brandished by the king's officers who searched and seized wherever their suspicions led them. Such a warrant, instead of circumscribing authority for a limited and proper purpose, served as a badge of legal authority for arbitrary intrusions. It was foremost among grievances impelling the struggle for independence.

Unreasonable searches and seizures are prohibited by the Constitution. A reasonable one—duly sanctioned after showing probable cause for it, or reasonable because of the circumstances apart from such sanction—is certainly allowed.

It should not be assumed that the protection declared by the Constitution had its origin there. Originally the English common law recognized no right at all for an invasion of a man's home. Gradually the intrusion gained recognition as a matter of public necessity—for the apprehension of criminals, and particularly for the recovery of stolen property. Warrants and writs conferred upon public authorities a right to intrude, limited to the necessity at hand. It is at making sure that such a right is not abused and such a limitation not exceeded that the Fourth Amendment and its state counterparts aim.

The protection which the Fourth Amendment gives has been incorporated in state constitutions. This is binding on the state, but not the **federal** government. The converse is true for the Fourth Amendment itself. By virtue of the Fourteenth Amendment, however, the **federal** guaranty in this portion of the Bill of Rights applies to acts of state officials as well. A violation of rights under the Fourth Amendment has been declared by the Supreme Court to result in a denial of due process of law and the exclusion of its illegal harvest is required in state prosecutions as well as **federal** (see p. 52 *supra*).

Acts by government officials and departments in all branches of government come within the purview of this protection. The acts of private persons are, of course, not within the scope of constitutional prohibitions. But instances where police took advantage of private intrusions to seize or search themselves have been held to constitute a violation of constitutional rights.

WHAT IS SECURED

What is guarantied is "the right of the people to be secure in their persons, houses, papers, and effects, against unreasonable searches and seizures." Specifically, what sort of things are protected?

The Person

Bodily searches are the most intrusive of all. Cases in which they are an issue typically involve persons suspected of hiding narcotics, of druken driving, of rape.

When there were facts justifying arrest based on suspicion of narcotics possession, a rectal examination by a physician under proper sanitary conditions was held not to be an unreasonable search.

Fluoroscopic examination of the stomach was followed by a laxative and then an emetic to recover narcotics previously swallowed, in another case. The person had not been arrested, but submitted to the procedure voluntarily after the dangers of leaving a packet of heroin in his stomach were explained to him. Again no violation of a constitutional right was found in obtaining the narcotics under these circumstances.

Where a blood sample was taken by a physician from an unconscious accident victim to determine the likelihood of intoxication, the absence of consent under the circumstances did not make this search and seizure a violation of constitutional rights.

But where a police officer performed chemical tests to determine the presence of blood on the penis of an unwilling man who had been lawfully arrested and charged with rape, violation of his rights was found by the court. A similar determination has been made in more than one case where the person arrested was subjected unwillingly to stomach pumping, though under proper medical conditions. The Supreme Court held in one such case that this procedure was so fundamentally objectionable that it was a denial of due process of law quite apart from being an unreasonable search and seizure.

A search of "the person" has been interpreted to mean a

search of his clothing, the contents of his pockets, and things under his immediate control. These things, rather than bodily content, are the frequent subject of claims of unreasonable search of the person.

When a lawful arrest is made, search of the person is a lawful incident of it. Examination of clothing and its contents are clearly proper, but the crucial question is what is under the immediate control of the person arrested. Coming to a man's home with a warrant for his arrest is not authorization to search his house. Yet the fact that he is not wearing his jacket when the arrest is made—it is lying on a chair nearby—does not exclude the jacket or its contents from a lawful search.

It is impossible to fix general rules for what is within the immediate control of a person arrested. Courts tend to find a greater range of immediate control when the place of arrest is public, or at least not the sort of place which is protected against unreasonable searches. This is logical since security of possessions require personal control over them in a public place, but not in a private place which is itself secure and therefore affording security for things within it. The problem is to avoid dissipating protection against unreasonable search of home or other protected place simply because an arrest is made there.

The Place

The term "houses" has been given broad interpretation in according protection.

Automobiles are protected places, though the standard for unreasonable search is quite different than in the case of a home. When a person drives his car on a public road, he is in a private, not public, place and the car is protected from arbitrary inspections and seizures of its contents. The same holds true when the unoccupied car stands parked in a public place. Because of its mobility, however, suspicious circumstances may make inspection of a car reasonable without obtaining a warrant for this purpose, while under the same suspicious circumstances an on-the-spot search of a home, without warrant, would be unreasonable.

In New York, the protection has been held to extend to a taxicab while in the hire of the person claiming protection, and it is safe to state that not ownership, but temporary use and possession is the requisite for a claim of protection.

Offices, stores, factories, and other places of business are all within the constitutional protection. Any place which is part of person's place of business is included.

The same view is taken with regard to dwellings. Barns and garages, for instance, are generally recognized as part of the home. When the facts indicate they are not part of the home, they are excluded from protection. Open land is protected if it is part of the homestead. But unfenced or unbounded land which is not treated as part of one's home generally is not protected.

Hotel rooms, if used as a home even temporarily, are protected. The single-day transient guest, living out of his suitcase, has been denied protection for his room in some cases, and accorded it in others. If the circumstances indicate an affirmative answer to the question "did he in any sense live there while he occupied the room?" protection is in order. The crucial consideration is the existence of some right to exclude the rest of the world, even though short-lived.

Buildings need not be occupied to be protected. The premises may be vacant. If they would be entitled to protection when occupied, they cannot be arbitrarily searched when unoccupied. The same reasonaing applies conversely, so that places abandoned to the world may be freely searched.

Boats and ships are protected. Less stringent standards are applied to determine the reasonableness of the search, from the same consideration of mobility which applies to automobiles.

The Thing

It is important to note that people are protected not only against search and seizure of property which they are legally entitled to possess. Things may be wrongfully in a person's possession—stolen goods, for instance—and the protection applies no less. It is invasion of privacy, not disturbance of property, which the law seeks to prevent. If showing that the property was stolen served to make lawful its earlier seizure, the police would enjoy the privilege of taking a calculated risk that a particular search might turn out to be reasonable, depending upon what it produces. What the Fourth Amendment seeks to prevent is police intrusion, mistaken or otherwise, unless such intrusion seems in advance to be reasonable under the circumstances. A search which may seem desirable to the police even when weighed against the risks of finding nothing, may be very far from reasonable.

"Papers" include every sort of written thing, business and personal, corporate and individual. To come within the protection, papers must belong to the person claiming it or be in his care. Either condition will suffice.

Public records, or papers of a sort in which the public has a legitimate interest, do not receive the same degree of protection for their privacy as do private papers. What may be an unreasonable demand for inspection or an unreasonable examination with regard to private papers may be quite reasonable when the papers are affected with a public interest. (See p. 83 *infra.*)

SECURITY FOR WHOM

The right to be secure against unreasonable searches and seizures may be asserted by anyone whose right of privacy is violated. Technical legal distinctions of property or contract law have no place in determining who is entitled to protection. The protection is not of a legal interest other than privacy, and the subtle distinctions appropriate to determine a question of right to possession of property has no place in determining whether the right of privacy of a person who has possession is violated.

In line with this, a search may violate the rights of more than one person—the owner of an article and the one in whose care he has left it, for example. If, however, a person simply has possession, without any sort of interest in the thing—a messenger boy, for instance—it is obvious that a search and seizure will not be an invasion of his privacy, and so not a violation of his **constitutional** right. Of course, such a person may still have a claim of unlawful search or seizure of his *person*, if the situation included such acts.

A person may have a firm and fundamental legal interest in property, and yet not be entitled to claim **constitutional** protection. A landlord normally would not be able to assert the illegality of search and seizure in an apartment or office which was leased. The tenant's privacy, but not the landlord's, was violated. The same result was reached where a husband had legal title to a house occupied by his estranged wife. The fact that he did not live there at all was what mattered. And where a group or association is so impersonal in its scope of membership and activities that it is not simply an extension of the private interests of its members, the right of individual members to be secure against unreasonable searches is not violated by a search of the group's papers.

The circumstances alone may import the privacy of one person into the property of another. Thus, although a wife had no legal interest in a house owned by her husband, a search of it was a violation of her privacy because of the relation of husband and wife. But a husband does not have a right of privacy with regard to his wife's body, at least not the sort which is violated by unreasonable searches. Only the wife may claim **constitutional** protection in this case.

An employee has a right of privacy at his place of employment. In one instance the employee's desk was searched by the police with the employer's permission. The court found that since the desk was given over to the employee for his exclusive use, the right to be free from searches was his to give up or insist upon, as he chose, and not his employer's.

When consent is given for a search, the protection otherwise available is waived. To be effective, consent must be freely given, and not result from any threats or other coercive devices, or from deceptions. It is not necessary to resist the entry of police officers who express their determination to conduct a search in order to refuse consent. But if the victim of the search is present, it is necessary that he indicate his unwillingness to be searched, otherwise consent may be construed from his acquiescence. The one whose privacy is jeopardized by the search is the only one who can consent (though he may do so through someone else who is authorized to express his consent). Obviously, where more than one person's privacy is at stake, failure to obtain consent from any one preserves that person's rights. Even husband and wife cannot give effective consent for searches which violate the other's privacy.

Only the person whose privacy has been violated may claim the protection. The fact that the wrongful consequences affect another person does not confer constitutional rights on that other person. Thus, if there is an unlawful search of one man's house and evidence of a crime committed by another man is obtained, the other man cannot avail himself of constitutional remedies by claiming that the evidence is the product of a violation of Fourth Amendment guaranties and must be suppressed. And the owner of the house, unless he is implicated in the crime, has no standing to demand such suppression.

It is important to recognize that the constitutional guaranty against unreasonable search applies to persons who have criminal records and are notorious as professional criminals in the same way that it applies to everyone else. Numerous times courts have held that the suspect's criminal notoriety does not make a search more reasonable. The independent probability that a crime has been committed, which may be indicated by various circumstances, is what is to be considered. The proven penchant for crime of the suspect is not a proper circumstance for such consideration. Although the police frequently find such niceties burdensome, our legal system cherishes a distinction between rights to be accorded one who does not stand convicted, and one who does.

Corporations are entitled to the protection of the Fourth Amendment. The concept of privacy for corporate affairs is somewhat different than for individuals, and intrusion into corporate privacy is considered more reasonable in many instances. The corporation is a creature of the state, and public authority which has created it reserves the right, to some extent, to look into its affairs. Particularly is this true when the corporation's business is largely a matter of public concern—public utilities being the extreme case.

All persons within the jurisdiction of the United States, aliens and citizens alike, are entitled to protection under the Fourth Amendment.

VIOLATION OF THE RIGHT

What Is A Search

What is in plain view of whomever cares to look cannot be the subject of a search. This is true even if the things seen are in a place protected from physical intrusion.

A number of cases have involved viewing the openly visible contents of locked automobiles from the outside. This is not a search, even when done with the aid of a flashlight beam. In one case involving a searchlight beam projected from one boat onto the deck of another, the Supreme Court said that such viewing was not a search, and as such was the same as observing through binoculars.

Many decisions have held that surveillance through windows or other regular building apertures from the outside does not constitute a search. If the blinds are not drawn, the things within are not being kept private from whomever cares to observe them.

Harder cases are presented when keyholes or other openings not normally closed for privacy are the means of observation. There is a strong tendency here to find that no search has occurred unless there was physical intrusion, in the case of seeing things as well as in the case of hearing them (see *supra,* pp. 48-51). But it is decided quite consistently that where the police have themselves made the opening for their observation, there is a physical intrusion and hence a search.

Perhaps the most delicate test to which these principles have been put is in the decision of a recent California case involving observation by an officer of the Long Beach Police Department at an amusement park in that city. A pipe extended through the roof above pay toilets, and when uncapped gave a view of two of the toilet booths to the officer on the roof. A regular watch for long hours was maintained in the hope of apprehending persons engaged in criminal homosexual activity, and the dedication of the police officer was rewarded one night by a view of the anticipated infamous crime against nature. In finding that this constituted an unlawful search, the court pointed out that this was not a preliminary inspection by one about to make an arrest for which he already had probable cause; that it was a general exploratory search conducted solely to find evidence of guilt, a practice condemned by both federal and state law (see p. 52 *supra*); and that an enclosed toilet booth, even though in a public toilet in a public amusement park, was a place of privacy for the occupant and entitled to the same protection as if it were in his home. The fact that the pipe was not installed by the police, and that the removal of its cap was outside the protected premises, made no difference.

Private Intrusions

An illegal search may be made by a private citizen, who obtains things which are valuable as evidence. He then turns them over to the police. Such evidence is properly available to the prosecution, since it is not produced by a violation of constitutional rights. No government official or agency has been in any way involved in an unreasonable search and seizure. It is against this, and not against unreasonable searches and seizures per se, that the Constitution affords protection. If there is any police participation in the search or seizure, however, even though the acts are initiated by a private citizen the interdiction of the Constitution applies.

Arrest

Generally speaking, a valid, lawful arrest is one made pursuant to a valid warrant (which is an authorization by a judicial officer, issued when he is convinced that there is probability of the criminal liability suspected); or made without warrant when there is an apprehension of crime by a police officer (subject to qualifications which need not detain us here).

Earlier in this chapter we mentioned the fact that searches incidental to valid arrest are reasonable and require no separate warrant. Frequently, however, the case is presented of an invalid arrest, a search in the course of it, and the discovery of evidence which, if discovered before the arrest, would have been a basis for the issuance of an arrest warrant. An attempt is then made to validate the arrest based on the evidence so discovered.

This will not work. To allow it would again make of Fourth Amendment protection something against which the police may take a calculated risk. The purpose of the amendment's guaranty is not to impose a risk on the police, but to forbid such acts, with or without attendant risk.

The suppresion of evidence seized by unlawful arrest extends to fingerprint and photograph records of the person arrested, and, as we have seen (p. 77 *supra*), the results of bodily examination. But suppressing such evidence is quite a different matter from destroying or surrendering the police records.

Inspections

Inspections are frequently made without legal formality, especially by local government officials. Typical subjects are buildings, equipment, goods, and activities, and the inspections are made in the interest of the health, safety, and general welfare of the community. Are these unreasonable searches?

The question is whether the right of the individual is to be sacrificed for the common good. When it is a device to serve other purposes beyond the inspector's scope of regulation in the public interest, the search and its products are illicit. Unusual practices in the conduct of such inspections will make them into unreasonable searches, and courts will require that warrants be obtained so that they are subject to justification in advance.

Since inspections of this sort are of matters normally lawful, some public urgency should be present to justify inspections without warrant of homes and other private places not in the usual field of regulation.

Orders To Produce For Examination

Judicial and administrative process may be employed as an equivalent of search and seizure. Constitutional protection is available against any abuse of such process which constitutes the equivalent of an unreasonable search and seizure.

The instrument of court process to compel the production of papers, books, records and other documents, or articles, is called a *subpoena duces tecum*. It may by be used to require production in court of evidence; or before some investigative body, such as a grand jury or legislative committee, production of things required for the purposes of conducting an investigation; or before some administrative agency of the government for purposes of investigation or regulation of matters within its jurisdiction. The subpoena is an order, disobedience of which will be punished. An order to produce certain things may be issued in the first instance by the body interested in examining them if that body is authorized by law to issue such orders.

It must be remembered that constitutional immunity protects against the acts of all parts of the government— one of which is the judicial system. Thus even a party to a civil suit who is ordered by a subpoena to produce certain things as evidence in court would have available constitutional protection if the order were unreasonable. Although such a subpoena is prepared and served by a private party on its own initiative, it is an instrument of the court and carries with it the court's authority. Therefore the constitutional guaranty limits its use.

As long as subpoenas are properly used for purposes for which they are designed in the administration of justice and the conduct of government they are not considered to be unreasonable, and hence are free of constitutional prohibition.

Two factors are most important in determining the propriety of these orders:

The first is the relevance to the proceedings of what is demanded. In this connection reasonable latitude is given for the exercise of discretion by the persons conducting the proceeding. They are presumed to be seeking what they need, even if it is not immediately apparent to others.

The other requirement is that the things to be produced be specified with sufficient particularity. Sweeping demands which will provide the opportunity to rummage through files to find out if there are things of interest in them are unreasonable searches.

These two limitations combine to prevent searches for evidence of guilt, which we have already noted to be a fundamental objective of Fourth Amendment protection (see *supra,* p. 52).

PROTECTION OF THE RIGHT

Warrant

Not all searches are unreasonable. Not all searches made without a warrant are unreasonable: the circumstances, and especially the fact that the search is incidental to a lawful arrest, may make it reasonable. If there are no such circumstances a warrant is required when places or things within the scope of the constitutional protection are searched, if the search is not to be condemned as unlawful.

The constitutional requirement that a warrant be issued only upon probable cause means that facts presented to the judicial officer authorized to issue warrants raise an honest belief in his mind, which is objectively reasonable, that the charge which is the reason for the search is valid.

These facts must be presented in the 'form of "oath or affirmation." Normally an affidavit must be made by the one who supplies the information which is the basis of the issuance of the warrant. Bare suspicions or accusations by a person which he is not prepared to stand behind personally cannot be the basis of a warrant, no matter how persuasive they may be.

A warrant must state with great detail the subjects of search and seizure, and the authority it confers is limited by this. This does not mean that each object which may be taken must be specified in advance. It does mean that the scope of the search and its results must be limited strictly to the purposes for which the warrant was issued, and that a sufficiently particular account be given in the warrant so that objects which are within the purview of the warrant may be readily distinguished from those which are not.

The detailed requirements for warrants issued by federal and state authorities are matters of federal and state law. Those laws, which differ in details, are governed ultimately by the search and seizure limitations of the federal and state constitutions.

Remedial Measures

Remedial measures for victims of illegal search and seizure take several forms:

The warrant under which the search is attempted may be attacked as invalid.

If there has been a seizure, an action designed to effect a return of what was taken may be commenced.

Civil liability exists for damages sustained as a result of unlawful search or seizure. A judicial officer or other person who issues a warrant without having legal authority to do so is liable for damages incurred in the execution of the warrant. An officer executing a warrant which is valid on its face, though in reality invalid, is protected from civil liability for damages. If a valid warrant is issued, but the search and seizure goes beyond what is authorized, the officers who made the excessive, unlawful, search are liable.

It should be noted that the search must be conducted without digression or dalliance, and once made cannot later be resumed. Many cases find illegality when these requirements are not strictly observed.

Various penal provisions covering illegal search and seizure are found in state statutory law. Although the law reports abound in cases in which such illegal acts of the police are an issue, the criminal courts of the country remain unburdened by prosecutions under these laws.

The inadmissibility of evidence illegally seized is generally recognized as the most effective brake on police violation of the Fourth Amendment and its state constitutional counterparts.

State law in about half the states excludes illegally seized evidence from a prosecution. Since 1961, all state prosecutions have been required to get along without such evidence, as have federal prosecutors since 1914 (see *supra,* p. 52).

The "fruit of the poisonous tree" doctrine is applied in support of the Fourth Amendment. A search may be unlawful, and what is seen, heard, or seized may not be admitted as evidence. But often such things provide clues for further investigation which produces desired evidence. Such evidence is likewise inadmissible. Once it has been plausibly alleged that evidence is tainted the prosecutor must show that the evidence was independently obtained without the proscribed aids, in order to gain admittance for the evidence.

Chapter 8

PRIVACY-FROM PROPERTY RIGHT
TO PERSONAL RIGHT

Technology and Privacy

The redefinition of protection of privacy over the past ten years has evolved principally around the issue of electronic surveillance. This had been a problem of increasing concern to civil libertarians and constitutional scholars but had not stirred the public consciousness until the Watergate revelations and the White House tapes became household words. As a result of Watergate, ordinary citizens, at least for a while, have been made aware of the ways in which their private lives and records can come under the scrutiny of unauthorized people. The development of surveillance technology, going as far back as the invention of the telephone and the telegraph, has slowly forced a reexamination and redefinition of privacy per se and made it absolutely necessary for the courts to reinterpret the Constitution in the light of these new techniques.

It might be useful to review the historical background of privacy. The framers of the Constitution, remarkable as they were, could function only in relation to their own experience and philosophy. When the Fourth Amendment was drafted in terms of the "right of the people to be secure in their persons, houses, papers and effects against unreasonable searches and seizures" its authors could not foresee the development of a technology that would transcend physical barriers like walls and roofs, space and distance. Private property, and the ownership thereof, were of vital importance; the right of the individual (male and white, to be sure) to enjoy immunity from state interference in the use and disposition of his property were the basic considerations that entered into the philosophy and phrasing of the Fourth Amendment.

Of similar importance to the authors of the Constitution were ideas of as much freedom as possible for the individual, balanced, of course, against the demands of the social order. The social order was likewise conceived of as a system in which the government intruded as little as possible in the affairs of its citizens. To secure these democratic rights and privileges, the First Amendment specifically enumerated the rights of freedom of speech, of the press, of assembly, and forbade the establishment of religion. The Third Amendment prohibited the quartering of soldiers in private homes during peacetime, partially to affirm the right of the individual to enjoy the privacy of his home without unwelcome intrusions over which he had no control. The Fourth Amendment, part of which is quoted above, guarantees citizens that they and their homes and possessions shall be safe from unreasonable search or seizure and if these intrusions were to take place, they should do so only with authorization of a warrant issued on the basis of probable cause. The Fifth Amendment can also be viewed as a protection for personal privacy in that it prohibits the state from compelling any individual to testify against himself and thus reveal personal information that he would prefer to be private.

These might be regarded as implicit protections that flowed from the framers' experience with European history and its long legacy of interference in the lives and property of individuals. More explicit were the long-standing common law protections against trespass, nuisance and eavesdropping. Protection was also afforded to certain confidential relationships and to the privacy of letters in the mail.

These constitutional guarantees did not mean that there could be no searches or seizures or other kinds of intrusions. Search warrants and entries into people's homes could be ordered by the courts as a function of a compelling state interest, if there was probable cause. This does not mean there were no abuses; there were many by both the police and the courts. Furthermore, the nature of social and community living in the United States, combined with a free press eager to reveal all, often made it extremely difficult for some of these protections to be enforced. Nonetheless, there was an acceptable balance, for most people, between privacy and control.

Although the telephone, the microphone, the dictaphone and fast photography, with all their rich potential for abuse, came along in the last years of the nineteenth century, there was very little judicial recognition that these devices, when tampered with deliberately, violated the traditional protections of the Fourth Amendment. As long as the prohibitions within that amendment were construed to have physical, tangible, property-based meanings, wiretapping or bugging could not be recognized as genuine intrusions. In the case of *Olmstead* v. *U.S.* (1928) the Supreme Court held that tapping the telephone of a bootlegger during prohibition was not search and seizure as described by the Fourth Amendment which, said the court "cannot be extended and expanded to include telephone wires reaching the whole world from the defendant's house or office." Actual physical trespass was still considered a requirement of the guarantees of the Fourth Amendment. Justice Brandeis wrote a famous dissent in this case advocating the idea of a constitutional right to privacy but his ideas were not truly accepted until many years later. At the same time the court failed to prevent the use of illegally obtained evidence -- even when it was the result of a physical entry or seizure -- in state courts.

The doctrine uphel in Olmstead remained largely un changed until the 1960s. In the cases that turned directly on the matter of electronic surveillance, physical penetration was still held to be the standard of judgment. Not until the case of *Wong Sun* v. *U.S.* (1963) did the court specifically state that verbal communications were subject to Fourth Amendment protections.

In 1967 the Supreme Court handed down two decisions that decisively changed the concept of what constituted search and seizure. Physical penetration was no longer necessary to be considered an intrusion. In the case of *Berger* v. *New York,* conversations recorded by concealed devices in the defendant's office were introduced as evidence in court. The court found that the eavesdropping was unconstitutional under the Fourth Amendment, and furthermore the New York statute that authorized the bugging was likewise unconstitutional because it had permitted indiscriminate listening without particular evidence in mind.

In *Katz* v. *United States* the FBI had attached a bugging device to the outside of a telephone booth from which the defendant, a California gambler and bookie, made his calls. In reversing the lower court decision, the Supreme Court held that the Fourth Amendment "protects people, not places. What a person knowingly exposes to the public, even in his own home or office, is not a subject of Fourth Amendment protection but what he seeks to preserve as private, even in an area accessible to the public may be constitutionally protected..." "The government's activities in electronically listening to and recording the petitioner's words violated the privacy upon which he justifiably relied while using the telephone booth and thus constituted a "search and seizure" within the meaning of the Fourth Amendment. The fact that the electronic device employed to achieve that end did not happen to penetrate the wall of the booth can have no constitutional significance." Thus the court authoritatively rejected the concept that physical penetration per se was essential to be considered a violation of the Fourth Amendment. The importance of these rulings lies in the fact enunciated by the court that conversations intended to be private can be regarded legitimately as property and as such can be seized. This equates electronic eavesdropping with intrusion and thus equivalent to a search within the prohibitions of the Fourth Amendment against unreasonable searches and seizures.

After 1967 the federal government and many state legislatures enacted statutes that spelled out in painstaking detail all requests for authorization to eavesdrop by any electronic method. These requirements include:
1. The need to procure evidence about particular offenses, and thus prevent fishing expeditions.
2. A description of the offense in question, the persons likely to be involved in its commission, the location to be bugged and the status of the person requesting the authorization.
3. A time limit on any particular tap or bug, or an application for an extension.

These are general specifications. The details vary from state to state while the federal government, not surprisingly, has the broadest authority since it contains the provision that surveillance can be allowed under certain circumstances in the interests of "national security." This provision was invoked by President Nixon and his colleagues as the justification for many of their clearly illegal actions,

The concept that binds together the various kinds of authorization to intercept is probable cause--the simple, effective concept that there exists a real and defensible reason for believing that illegal action has been or is being committed. The term goes right back to the original wording of the Fourth Amendment which states unequivocally that "no warrants shall issue but upon probable cause, supported by oaths and affirmations and particularly describing the place to be searched and the person or things to be seized."

It's an interesting exercise in the study of the evolution of the court's thinking about the Fourth Amendment-and in effect the reflection of changing social values--to trace the history from Olmstead through Katz. The Olmstead case restated the traditional philosophy that actual physical intrusion had to take place, and that "tangible effects" had to be seized. Despite vigorous dissent from certain members of the court, the majority refused to yield on the physical, or property-based notion of privacy. Thus, voices traveling along a tapped telephone were not considered subject to the same protections as a voice inside a house being overheard by a person hidden in the house for the express purpose of eavesdropping. Although the concept of a constitutional right to privacy was strongly presented by Justice Brandeis in his dissenting opinion, the time apparently was not quite ripe for acceptance by the conservative majority of the court.

In the case of *Goldman* vs. *United States* in 1942, the issue turned on whether a detectaphone placed against the wall of the defendant's office violated the Fourth Amendment. The court applied the Olmstead doctrine that the object had not actually penetrated the wall and therefore did not constitute physical entry. In the case of *Silverman* vs. *United States,* in 1961, the bugging device was a spike mike that did actually penetrate the wall and touched a heating duct that picked up conversations and transmitted them to outside listeners. In this instance, the court held that this constituted an actual physical penetration of the premises and this did violate the Fourth Amendment. Thus the court inched slowly toward redefining the concept of privacy and establishing it as a constitutional right guaranteed to individuals rather than a function of property. The Wong Sun, Berger, and Katz cases previously discussed completed the transition.

After Katz and Berger

The Katz and Berger decisions gave the highest judicial authority to the idea of a constitutional right of privacy. However, within a year after the ruling in these cases, Congress passed the Omnibus Crime Control and Safe Streets Act of 1968, part of which effectively undercut protections recognized by the Katz and Berger rulings. The national temper was becoming increasingly aggrieved by the rising crime rate, the demonstrations and general unrest of the late 1960s. "Law and order" was being promoted as the catch phrase of the times, prompting Congress to enact anticrime legislation that had some very regressive features.

Title III of the act was the first federal law to regulate wire-tapping and electronic surveillance. Although the law was theoretically drafted in conformance with the constitutional principles of Katz and Berger, it in fact circumvents them to a large degree. It may well be that Congress was responding to pressures to utilize electronic surveillance techniques (in fact, any surveillance methods) in the war against crime and not allow constitutional requirements to interfere with the apprehension of criminals

Although the law bans "the interception and disclosure of wire or oral communications" there are a few significant exceptions to this overall prohibition. Among these exceptions to this overall prohibition. Among these exceptions was the right granted to federal, state and local officials to apply to a federal judge for a court order permitting wire-tapping and bugging in the investigation of a wide range of activities including the standard practices of organized crime and more mundane offenses such as marijuana use, civil disorder, and obstruction of a criminal investigation. Many states allow an even more flexible interpretation of those offenses for which electronic surveillance may be authorized upon application to a state judge. There are, without question, more safeguards to privacy than there were before the Katz and Berger decisions but they have been substantially diluted by the provisions of the Omnibus Crime Control Act. Improperly obtained evidence will still be suppressed or excluded in any trial or hearing if it can be proved that the interception failed to comply with the provisions of the statute. In actual fact, however, it would be extremely difficult for anyone to prove that a government eavesdropper did not have some kind of statutory justification for his actions.

National Security

One of the more ominous provisions of the act was Section 2511 (3) that declined to "limit the constitutional power of the President to take such measures as he deems necessary to protect the nation against actual or potential attack or other hostile acts of a foreign power, to obtain foreign intelligence information deemed essential to the security of the United States, or to protect national security information against intelligence activities. Nor... to protect the United States against the overthrow of the government by force or other unlawful means, or against any other clear and present danger to the structure and existence of the government." Under this section, communications intercepted under presidential authority were allowed to be received in evidence. This broad ranging sanction gave the government carte blanche to use all kinds of electronic surveillance without a court order simply by invoking the magic words, national security. One of the by-products of this statutory permissiveness was the complex happening called Watergate.

Under the Nixon administration there occurred almost every possible abuse of individual or institutional privacy. Operatives working for the Committee to Reelect the President opened the official proceedings by breaking into the offices of the Democratic National Headquarters with the intention of taking papers from the files and leaving bugging equipment behind them. In the course of investigating this event discovery was made of telephone taps on private citizens, the breaking into and entering of a psychiatrist's office to secure evidence to be used against a former patient involved in litigation with the government and, most striking of all, the fact that the president of the United States himself taped all conversations held in his office without the knowledge of the other persons party to the conversation. This self-bugging device ironically backfored with such a vengeance that was probably the single most important factor in bringing down the Nixon presidency. The range of intrusions contemplated by the president's men was truly awesome; most of them involved wiretapping, bugging and the use of various kinds of nonpolitical dossiers for political purposes. One of the plans discussed entailed the use of income tax information from the files of the Internal Revenue Service to try to discredit political opponents. Other plans called for widespread bugging of private homes and hotel rooms in order to obtain information that might possibly be used against people who were considered enemies of the administration.

When these incidents or plans became public, members of the administration fell back on the catch phrase of "national security" to justify their most outrageous intrusions. Perhaps the most ominous threat to privacy, in fact to all forms of personal freedom, was a clandestine surveillance plan on a massive scale designed by the Nixon administration, using secret, warrantless surveillance machinery to gather private information about thousands of individuals and groups to be used when and if the president and his colleagues chose to employ it for their own ends.

This scheme was so extensive and so clearly unconstitutional that the FBI refused to participate in it. This system was all the more frightening in its implications because it was building up political files, not in an attempt to deal with actual violations of law, but as a deterrent to legitimate political actions guaranteed by the First Amendment. For a brief time America was moving toward 1984 and a world where privacy would be abolished. We may still be on the way, but no longer with official White House sanction. One lesson to be drawn from the whole Watergate saga should be a healthy caution toward the tools people employ to gain control over other people. The White House tapes will go down in history as a classic example of the servant destroying the master.

Personal Privacy -- Expanding the Concept

The case of *Griswold* v. *Connecticut* illustrates most graphically the transition of the idea of privacy from a propertybased concept to one of personal right. This case involved the dissemination of information about birth control devices by the Planned Parenthood League of the state of Connecticut to married couples who wished to receive this information. The case had been heard in Connecticut and the state contended that the defendants had violated Connecticut's statute barring the sale of contraceptives or offering advice about their use.

The defendants were twice convicted of violating the statute before it was heard by the Supreme Court. The Court ultimately reversed the state's decision on the fundamental grounds that the statute violated the sanctity of marital privacy. The Constitution does not, of course, enumerate marital privacy as one of its sacred guarantees. The various justices who wrote opinions on the issue used as their guiding principle the concept of personal liberties as being implicit in the amendments to the Constitution and thus applicable to the idea of marital privacy, even though marital privacy is not explicitly mentioned in the First, Fourth or Ninth Amendments.

Justice Douglas, who wrote the opinion for the court, held that specific guarantees in the Bill of Rights allowed the assumption that other guarantees could be derived from them although they were not specifically designated by name. This idea creates "zones of privacy" in an individual's life into which the state has no right to intrude unless there is a compelling state interest. In the case of *Griswold* v. *Connecticut* the court could not see that the state had an interest so compelling that it had the right to regulate the choice of a married couple to practice birth control by whatever methods they saw fit. This majority decision expanded the whole concept of the individual's constitutional right to make decisions about his or her personal life and actions without arbitrary interference by the state. It similarly reinforced the theme of the privacy of the home as a place where constitutionally protected activity may take place.

As an outgrowth of the principles enunciated in *Griswold* v. *Connecticut,* the logical next issue concerned distinctions between the behavior of married and unmarried people. This revolved around the assumption that the right to use contraceptives is constitutionally guaranteed and that discrimination between married and unmarried people as to their use would be unconstitutional.

The issue was tested by a well known birth control advocate, William Baird, who distributed contraceptive materials before a large audience of students. The Commonwealth of Massachusetts and the appeals court held that Baird had violated a state statute barring the distribution of contraceptives to unmarried persons. The Supreme Court (*Eisenstadt* v. *Baird*) reversed the decisions and stated that the statute did not have a compelling purpose; it did not enforce moral behavior by its restrictions and it violated the equal protection clause of the Fourteenth Amendment by treating married and unmarried people differently. The court held that the Griswold decision protected more than the marital relationship alone. It extended protection to include people who had a significant personal relationship and desired to choose for themselves, free from state pressures, whether or not they wanted to beget children.

Privacy and Personal Choice -- Roe v. Wade

In 1973 the Supreme Court decided a case that involved very strongly held emotional and constitutional issues. The above-mentioned cases paved the way for this decision which gave to both married and unmarried women the constituionally protected right to have an abortion. The principles derived from both the Griswold and Eisenstadt decisions were reinforced in *Roe* v. *Wade:* namely that subject to considerations of the health of the mother and the viability of the fetus, a woman has the right to terminate a pregnancy without interference from the state. In reviewing the decisions and precedents that led to the decision in *Roe* v. *Wade,* it becomes quite clear that given the Court's attitudes, over the last fifty years, toward the home, marriage and family that not even a matter as explosive as *Roe* v. *Wade* could have been decided differently at this time. The court has tended to regard family behavior and beliefs as fundamental rights that cannot be breached except in the presence of a compelling public interest. The decisions in Griswold and Eisenstadt reinforced the individual's right to make choices affecting his personsl life without the threat of governmental interference. The opinion in *Roe* v. *Wade* reflected the direction in which national social thinking has been moving - but it may not always be this way.

Although *Roe* v. *Wade* did legalize abortion per se, it left many issues that have not yet been resolved or may be reopened. At this writing, a physician in Massachusetts has been convicted of manslaughter because he did not take steps to protect the life of an aborted fetus that the state prosecutor later declared to be viable. The case will be appealed and the court will be asked to decide exactly when viability starts and when abortion becomes manslaughter. Since the question of when life begins has been debated by philosophers and theologians since the world began, it may be extremely difficult for even the Supreme Court of the United States to pinpoint the exact momen in time when life begins. Many groups are actively seeking to force a reconsideration of *Roe* v. *Wade* or to put forth a similar case that would result in a more congenial ruling. If that fact should come to pass, the expanded privacy concepts of the last few years may be due for a period of contraction and revision that would signal the return to a much more limited view of the right of privacy.

The determining factors in the court's decision in this controversial case sprang ultimately from the court's view of abortion as a right of privacy. Other factors, apart from the questions raised above, involve the right of the woman's physician to make an overriding medical decision on her behalf, and the rights of the potential father. In Massachusetts in 1974 a potential father did obtain a temporary injunction against his wife to prevent her from having an abortion. The court, however, ruled that a woman could not be compelled to bear a child against her will because its father wished her to do so. There are other issues requiring further exploration that were generated by this decision but they are not necessarily germane to the subject of privacy.

Technology and Civil Liberty

The growth of data banks and vast computerized pools of information about people in every aspect of their lives (discussed in part in Chapter 2) is probably the single most important element in the contemporary range of concerns about the right of privacy.

There is certainly no question that a sizable percentage of this banked information is either benevolent or at least neutral in terms of privacy. The blessings of technology are evident in areas like computerized medical information and records, rapidly accessible data for economic and urban planning, pooled cataloging information and information retrieval systems for libraries, airline and hotel reservations and charge account and subscription billing and payment records. Computer technology and allied electronic gadgetry has, like fire, a greater potential for good than for evil but it must be watched constantly.

While most data is gathered for gainful human and social purposes, the mere existence of this vast reservoir of personal information about individuals constitutes a covert invitation to misuse. Law enforcement agencies must necessarily collect a great deal of information about people to combat crime effectively, the army intelligence establishment maintains extensive files on people, often with very little justification. Often army and government surveillance have extended to organizations and individuals engaging in perfectly lawful activities. The political context of the late sixties may have tended to cloud the judgment of various agency officials and caused them to extend their file building further than it should have been pushed, even at a time of widespread political unrest. The danger of indiscriminate dossier-building is clearly to deter sincere citizen efforts to exercise their constitutional rights in pursuit of political goals.

The FBI, through its National Crime Information Center, maintains ever-expanding files that are rapidly being integrated into a nationwide network accessible to all law enforcement agencies and potentially to other groups or individuals, such as prospective employers, who are interested in discovering information outside their purview. An equally troublesome concomitant is the fact that the information in the file may be neither accurate nor current but since it is not regularly reviewed, the recipient of information about a particular person would tend to regard it as immutable fact.

A similar difficulty derives from the incomplete nature of some of the information, particularly in the area of arrest records. A dossier might well contain the information that a given individual was arrested on criminal charges and sentenced to three months in prison. This might be factually correct. What is not revealed, however, is the equally important explanation that the arrest took place during an antiwar demonstration or a desegregation rally and the charges were later thrown out, or the statute that permitted the arrest overturned. Readers of the record are not always equipped or even motivated to verify the accuracy of what they read. The simple fact that the information appears in somebody's file constitutes an evaluation in itself. Analogous to the arrest records of antiwar demonstrators are the records of those persons arrested for possession of marijuana or even being present where it was being used. Many of these charges were dismissed and in many states the statutes under which the arrest took place were invalidated. But it is probably safe to say that the ultimate disposition of these cases is not recorded in thousands of files. Therefore the arrest record remains with possible prejudicial effects for the rest of a person's life.

The degree to which the unofficial dissemination of dossier material had gotten out of hand was demonstrated by the decision in the case of *Menard* v. *Mitchell,* in 1971. A federal district court in Washington, D.C. forbade the FBI to disseminate criminal history records for use in determining employment or licensing acceptability, even though the requesting organization was a state or municipal law enforcement agency. The judge's opinion states among other comments: "arrest record material is incomplete and hence often inaccurate"; "No procedure exists to enable individuals to obtain, supplant, or to correct the criminal record information being used against them"; "Control of the data will be made more difficult and opportunities for improper use will increase with the development of centralized state information centers to be linked by computer to the Bureau."

The FBI, through its Security and Confidentiality Committee, drew up guidelines that were intended to determine the nature and scope of the information that could be disseminated and to whom it could legally be disseminated. The criminal history files were to be separate from files that contained other kinds of information such as juvenile violations, minor offenses, medical histories and nullified conviction records. Dissemination was to be limited only to law enforcement agencies; furthermore, the individual would have the right to see and challenge the information in his record. While the FBI endorsed these guidelines, they are not embodied in law or protected by administrative regulations.

Although the courts have been traditionally wary of interfering with the disposition of criminal data, increasing judicial notice is being taken of the problem. This concern may well have been triggered by the growth of databanks and the expanding potential for the abuse of information contained therein. The ever-spiraling crime rate underscores the need for comprehensive and rapidly accessible criminal information but in no way diminishes the need to balance the individual's control of personal information against the state's need to know. In the case of *Menard* v. *Mitchell,* the federal district court of the District of Columbia held among other opinions that the FBI was "without authority to disseminate arrest records outside the Federal government for employment, licensing or related purposes whether or not the record reflects a later conviction." As a result of this ruling the FBI did comply with the demand that it stop disseminating information to local and state agencies for employment and licensing checks.

However, it was not happy with the decision and called for remedial legislation. A sympathetic senator attached the desired piece of legislation to another bill in the form of a rider which was passed by voice vote. The FBI won back its lost privileges to disseminate information to anyone it chose for one more year but the issues raised by *Menard* v. *Mitchell* and whole problem of data banks will remain subjects for public and legislative concern for many years to come. The threats to privacy inherent in the existence of comprehensive, easily transmittable records cannot be resolved by existing constitutional doctrines or legislative remedies.

Several commentators on the privacy issues discussed here have proposed extremely detailed and inclusive recommendations both statutory and administrative in nature. They cover the kinds of material to be collected, review procedures to insure currency and accuracy, and provisions for expungement of data, tight safeguards on the dissemination of data and provisions for the data subject to see his own files. These proposals have all been made many times over but they have never been solidly legitimated by law.

On the state level, the New York Department of Motor Vehicles boasts one of the most sophisticated computerized record-keeping systems currently operational. It covers a wide spectrum of necessary information including license and registration files, insurance data, accident histories, scheduling of hearings for traffic violations, and medical information. While the computerization has undoubtedly increased the efficiency of the department's operations, certain of its procedures have raised civil libertarian hackles. The department is authorized by law to sell copies of its vehicle registrations to the highest bidder who then analyzes the information therein and prepares lists for sale to advertisers. This thriving commercial enterprise nets the state a sizeable income, as does its sale of registry information to credit and insurance companies. In 1967 a New York state resident brought suit against the state alleging that the sale of registry information to private users was unconstitutional *(Lamont* v. *Commissioner of Motor Vehicles)*. Lamont further charged that the actions of the state and company to whom it sold information were "in violation of the plaintiff's right of privacy and constitute a deprivation of liberty and property under the 1st, 4th, 9th and 14th Amendments."

The court ruled against the plaintiff saying in effect that the information was a matter of public record. It is further possible and perfectly legal for any credit company or individual to buy print-outs of registry information for automobile and life insurance checks. Many states regard this information as confidential and prohibit its sale. In 1969 the New York State Senate Subcommittee on the Right of Privacy conducted hearings into the department's commercial arrangements and recommended that the state law be changed to prohibit the sale of this kind of information. At this writing, the law has not yet been altered.

Along with all the other dossiers enumerated above and in Chapter 2, the political data bank has been a growing concern. Since the days of the Russian Revolution the United States government has compiled information by whatever means available on homegrown communists, suspected Communists, random radicals, leftists who happened to be in the wrong place at the wrong time and very respectable, and determinedly nonCommunist liberal individuals whose views or associations seemed questionable to the FBI or the Justice Department or local police departments. Infiltration and paid political informing have been standard methods of monitoring alleged subversive behavior. The fruits of this kind of information gathering were displayed for the world to see during the hysteria of the McCarthy era. Reputations and livelihoods were destroyed by charges and denunciations based on the reports of political informers whose evaluations helped create the dubious Attorney General's List of Subversive Organizations. After the defusing of Senator McCarthy, political vigilantism was on the wane, and political informing assumed a low profile for several years. It returned in full bloom during the civil rights drives of the early 1960s and the antiwar activities and demonstrations of the later years of the decade. The FBI and the various branches of the armed services charged with intelligence responsibilities have accumulated extensive files, in which photographs play a significant role, about people who have been in any way connected with expression of political dissent. An individual who was present on the edges of a peace rally might someday learn to his dismay that he is preserved in government files as a possible subversive or rabblerouser. Most recently, the FBI has come under sharp criticism for its tactics during these years.

One of the obvious dangers of political file building is that political files can easily shade over into other areas. The information contained in these dossiers can be leaked to investigative agencies, credit bureaus, prospective employers; in some cases to the media or to compatible political groups. There is no legislative or executive mandate for the collection of political intelligence. Various law enforcement agencies have taken it upon themselves, with the encouragement and support of the FBI, to gather political intelligence as a function of law enforcement. Political dossiers, however, are not used as specific law enforcement tools, but more often to embarrass people who have taken part in any activity that might be construed as nonestablishment and to discourage them from exercising their First and Fourth Amendment rights.

Information files about individuals have been part of industrial society for a long time. Long before computers revolutionized the technology of record keeping, government, businesses, social service organizations, schools and the like maintained historical records about people that were often quite detailed and comprehensive. It has been one of the fundamental interests of students of the data bank phenomenon to discover whether the data collected by computer techniques differs in quality as well as quantity from that gathered and maintained in manual records. There may be little point in speculating about whether the drive for information spurred the technology or whether the beckoning computer whetted the appetite for expanding information. In any case, it seems that the possibility of easily and cheaply storing more information is steadily if slowly broadening the kinds of information that are finding their way into the data banks. Although a great many people are deeply concerned about the abuse potential of dossiers and data banks in all areas of life, the scope of collecting and distribution still appears to be largely discretionary. Until such time that there are substantive legal safeguards to control the use of stored data, the dangers of serious violations of personal privacy will continue to be a problem in American society.

The Privacy Act of 1974

Any taxpayer has noted on his 1040 package this year a reference to the Privacy Act of 1974. That act provides that each federal agency inform individuals whom it asks to supply information, of

1) the authority for the solicitation of the information;

2) whether disclosure of such information is mandatory or voluntary;

3) the principal purpose or purposes for which the information is to be used;

4) the routine uses which may be made of the information;

5) the effects on the individual of not providing the requested information.

The form then goes on to relate in its notification to each of the foregoing items.

While the Privacy Act will not operate as a total panacea for governmental invasions of privacy, it does set ground rules for government agencies which should at least offer some protection against arbitrary gathering and misuse of personal information at the federal governmental level. How successful the implementation of the legislation will be remains to be seen.

INDEX

Abortion, 99-100
Accountants, 57-58
Advertising, 1, 2, 3, 11, 17
Arrest, 78, 85
Attorneys, 59-60

Banks, 30-31
Biography, 15, 16, 19-20
Broadcasts, 1, 4, 6, 17

Census information, 74
Comic strips, 11, 15
Computers, 25-26
Confidential business facts, 72-73
Consent, 4, 50, 81
Copyright, 67
Corporate names, 12, 13
Court proceedings, 4, 6, 20, 21
Credit bureaus, 26, 27
Customer lists, 71

Data banks, 25-26, 103-104
Debt collection, 22-24
Detectophone, 44, 49
Direct mail, 29-30
Divulgence, 45
Doctors, 62-63

Eavesdropping, 48-53
Employer's confidence, 69
Employers, informing, 23
Endorsements, 1, 2
Evidence of guilt, 62, 84
Exposed Mail, 32-33

Fair Credit Reporting Act, 26-28
Federal Communications Act, 38, 41-48

Fictitious names, 12
Fiduciary relations, 73
Fourth Amendment, 48, 75, 90 et seq

Hidden transmitter, 50
Husbands and wives, 60-62, 81, 82

Impersonation, 3
Inadmissibility, 42, 46, 48, 51
Incidental use, 16
Income tax returns, 74
Indecency, 8, 20
Inspections, 26, 85
Interception, 44

Journalists, 58-59

Magazines, 5, 7, 8, 10, 15, 19, 20, 21
Mail, 32-37
Mail watch, 34-36
Medical communications, 62
Medical data, 8, 21-22, 63
Merged name, 12
Minifon, 50
Moving pictures, 6, 11, 12, 14, 16, 22

Names, 1-17 passim
National Security, 96-97
Newspapers, 8, 15, 21
Novels, 7, 11, 14

Obscurity, 5
Omnibus Crime Control & Safe Streets Act, 95

Patent, 67
Peeping Tom laws, 24
Personal disgrace, 56
Personality, 1-17 passim
Physical examinations, 77
Physical intrusion rule, 50
Pictures, 1-17 passim
Police records, 9, 21
Political activities, 55
Portraits, 1-17 passim
Privacy Act of 1974, 106
Protection papers, 80, 81, 86
Protected persons, 80-83
Protected places, 51, 78
Protected property, 79
Prying, 33-34
Psychologists, 59
Publicity, 2, 7
Public interest, 4-9, 14-17
Public officials, 5
Public papers, 3

Religious beliefs, 55

Religious confessions, 63-64

Search warrants, 87
Searches and seizures, 50, 76, 90
    et seq
Self-incrimination, 56
Sender, 46
Shadowing, 24
Spike mike, 49
Subpoena duces tecum, 86
Surveillance, 24, 83

Technology, 90 et seq
Telegraph, 3, 22, 37-39
Telephone, 3, 41-48
Trade names, 13
Trade or advertising use, 10, 14-17
Trade secrets, 50, 65-72
Twinfon, 45

Vote, 56

Wiretapping, 41-48